Derra was born into this world with a rare disorder which dealt her a uniquely twisted hand in life. Awesome adventures with her squad intertwined with personal demons. The white noise tried to break her down, but she's decided to blast it away and see the beauty in her life and this gorgeous world.

Dear Beach,

Warm sand scrunching between your toes... cool white foam lined waves crashing on the current... hot Vitamin-D rays beaming down from a clear blue universe... floating sphere of fire setting as a glowing luminosity rises... crackling pit of flames sparking into the darkness while genuine conversations fill the breeze over cold coronas...

We all need that one place where we can truly unwind and unplug from the daily madness that adds to our everlasting insomnia. A place where every worry, fear, doubt and concern slips into a coma. A place where technology isn't allowed to be super-glued to our hands and eyes.

We all need that unscheduled time where the only responsibilities to be accounted for are laughter from inside jokes amongst family and friends... creating memories to add to our lanes... one too many over stuffed s'mores being inhaled... walks along the waves indulging in the beautiful scenery of endless ocean... becoming mesmerized by the faceted ombre sunset painted on Mother Nature's canvas...

What I just described to you is my sanctuary. Dull or boring are never scheduled on my calendar, but days of escaping are. Beach... this one syllable word is my morphine that numbs the chaos of the constant insanity that my mind is shifted into. I have no worries when sand and ocean are in the presence of my eyes. I feel like myself instead of the version that's expected. This is the one place where I can just be.

Derra Nicole Sabo

DEAR YOU

AUSTIN MACAULEY
PUBLISHERS LTD.

ISBN 9781786293077 (Paperback)
ISBN 9781786293084 (Hardback)
ISBN 9781786293091 (E-Book)
www.austinmacauley.com

First Published (2017)
Austin Macauley Publishers Ltd.
25 Canada Square
Canary Wharf
London
E14 5LQ

Acknowledgments

To my family… This one's for you. My life would be very boring without all of the awesome insanity you bring to the party. I also wouldn't be the person that I am at this moment. I love y'all!

This book is dedicated to those who live in a
World of words.
To those whose megaphones have
Silenced themselves due to social difficulties.
Whether they flow from your
Heart or mind,
In written or lyrical form,
Here's to you…

Dear You,

How y'all doin'? Perfectly imperfect I hope. Well, I come to you today because I have a favor to ask of you. I need you to do me a kindness. Don't worry, it won't take up much of your time and it doesn't cost a single shiny Lincoln, however, it does require a few ounces of brain power and an open space in your heart. I have a story for you... Yes, I know what you're thinking, "Oh great, another book about a nobody's life. A tale of how a nobody had a great childhood then hit a pot hole or two while growing up, but in the end found herself and had a happily ever after." Well congrats, you are 50% correct. This is indeed a tale of a nobody's life, however, the bits about finding herself and having a happily ever are slightly off. My tale is about a young girl born with an unwanted label cemented onto her forehead, a label that cast a beautiful curse upon her heart. Do you know what it feels like to be a happy kid and then to have that rug pulled from under your feet? To go from feeling broken to damaged to completely worthless in one swift motion? How about wanting so much to fit in that it starts to break you down into a reflection that your 20/20 vision can no longer make out? To be marked as "different"?

I have a story to tell you, a story filled with happiness drowned out by brokenness, sprinkled with darkness and topped with a delicious suicide attempt. Served alongside is a refreshing shot of completely losing one's self, ending in rebuilding an underdog to become an invincible version of a beautifully imperfect human.

So here we are; just you and I sitting in a cozy place getting ready for the story that I have to tell. Now whether you listen or not is your decision...

Ok...ready? I'm going to jump almost 30 years into the future, well it would be the future for you since we don't know one another yet. So wait, hold up, I guess I'm starting you off in my present... Yep, we'll go with that. Less confusion. I'm beginning you at my present and we shall travel back together through the madness. Sounds good.

Three months before the big day (aka turning 30), I wrote several letters to my family and friends reminiscing down memory lane. Each one kissed with personal touches of memorable moments, lessons impressed into myself and lessons that I hope I impressed into their hearts. Confessions released (I figured it's safe to release some evidence due to the statute of limitation now being up), laughter turned into spontaneous smiling and tears stubbornly shed. All these snippets of my life and mind locked away in a long white paper rectangle labeled "My last kiss goodnight". Now I'm assuming that after reading this you have a possible conclusion swimming around your brain and if that conclusion is that I wrote out letters to my family along with my "last wishes" then you'd be right. A moment of my heart palpitating led my white knuckled hands to make sure that my loved ones were prepared just in case the Grim Reaper and I decided to throw an afterlife party.

So here I am sharing a few shining pieces of these letters about the people that protect my stitched scars. Embrace its honesty and pass on its contagiousness.

Dear Lu,

Wow, you and I have had quite the continuous adventure. Almost 21 years of laughter, getting caught causing chaos, moments of unexpected delirium and a few blow out fights. Everything a perfectly imperfect sister relationship should consist of. I will never forget the day you were born. I was so stoked to be a big sister. Aspirations to hopefully be a good role model for you to look up to and be a best friend that you could confide in. You were the cutest and tiniest human being I had ever seen.

Officially enrolled in Big sister Boot Camp... No longer being the only kid taking up residence in the Sabo house did require a touch of adjusting. Learning to share the attention and learning how to take care of another human being. I felt like mom's apprentice. Soaking in the techniques of a successful diaper change, getting the entire spoonful of food in your mouth and not your face (I think I averaged about 80% in that department... not too shabby). Learning how to turn those saddened tears into joyous smiles and that a swaying rocking motion implemented while singing a soft lullaby helps calm you into a wonderful slumber.

Witnessing you grow a little more each day was one of the coolest experiences I've had in my young life. Our memory lane is bumper to bumper. It's nearly impossible to pick which way to turn. Left...I'm turning left chica.

Houston, we have a problem... I will never forget the first time I babysat you...Oh My Goodness! I think you could sense my nervousness because you cried the entire time that Mom and Dad were out. Well, you did stop about 20 minutes before they came home, but before that I tried everything to calm you down. I read to you, sang to you (which probably made things a touch worse...lol). I played one of your favorite Barney videos (so much for Barney), I held you, rocked you back and forth in my arms, and even placed you in your swing thinking that the swaying motion would help. Then it happened... you stopped crying. I accidently stepped on you toy duck and its quacking distracted you enough to where you stopped crying. You had this fluffy stuffed duckling that when squeezed made a quacking sound.

"Quack, quack, quack" ...I squeezed that bird repeatedly until Mom and Dad got home...20 minutes of nothing but "quack". It gave me a headache, but it also made your frown turn upside down and that's all that mattered. After that, babysitting was a breeze. And I always made sure that there were fresh batteries in that duck, just in case.

Caribbean Splash Juice... Anytime Mom would buy that juice at the market, I would drink that stuff until it was gone. I came home from school one particular afternoon and as I entered the house you busted at the seams with excitement that I was home. I thought you had gone crazy or something. It was like your pants were filled with jumping beans. Turns out that that morning Mom had bought some of my favorite juice and you were very excited to bring it to me when I got home. You opened the fridge, grabbed the pitcher of juice and started towards me when...SPLASH! As the pitcher fell to the floor, your eyes filled with tears. A pool of juice surrounded you as you stood there holding the lid in your hands. Mom grabbed the pitcher, poured the little bit of juice that didn't spill out into a glass and handed it to you. You walked over to me, still crying and handed me the glass.

"Here you go DoDo..."

"Awe... thank you LuLu...Mmmm. That's good juice. Did you make it?"

A very tearful "Yes" was all you could say. Mom told you not to worry about it; that everything was alright. Then doing what I do best, I made you laugh by asking you if we should put our swimsuits on and go swimming in our new pool in the kitchen...giggles were had and tears were wiped away. Even as a youngster your heart was as big as the endless skies.

Roomies!... Mom and Dad were redecorating my room as a birthday gift to me, I believe I was 11. Anyways, all my furniture was placed in the center of my room while dad painted the walls. My bed however, was placed in your room and for the next week, you and I were now roomies. My bed was on one side of the room and your crib was on the other. Every morning you would throw or as you put it "share" one of your toys at me to wake me up. So kind to share your toys with me ;)

I would look at you in a sleepy haze and say that it wasn't time for me to get up yet. Then one Saturday morning I didn't get a toy tossed at me, instead your face was all up in bubble as you announced your presence. You had turned into a little escape artist. You figured out how to climb over the crib and get yourself out. The world was no longer safe... people would no longer be allowed to sleep in... Alyssa was loose. I think I told you to go visit Mom and Dad so that I could go back to sleep. Never a dull moment. I was happy when Dad was finished painting and I was able to move back to my room, but then I was quickly reminded that you could escape your crib the very next morning. Your first stop was my room, then Mom and Dad's. Nothing like a 7 am wake up call roaming the house.

School bound... you were (are) such a smart little cookie in school and in general. From elementary to high school, every afternoon was filled with all the happenings of your day. Who did what, who said what. It was like The Young and The Restless: junior edition. I knew everything about everyone. Stories shared while you did your homework and had your snack. Homework was always easy with you. We would get home and you would automatically start in. I hardly ever helped, but I was always there when you needed it. I do however recall a few weekends being spent indoors working on last minute projects or reports with you. Procrastination was a downfall for you. A few Saturday mornings were started off with the words, "Derra, I have a report due on Monday. Will you help me? Please."

You and I would cram in 2 weeks' worth of work in just two days and each time I would try to explain to you that waiting until the last minute rarely works. You always came to me and due to those puppy-dog eyes of yours, I was there. Until it happened… The last "last minute" report I helped you on. It was your Oregon Trail report. As you researched, I typed. While I drew out the diagram, you colored it in. As we finished I told you that this was the last time I was going to spend my weekend working on your reports. The word "Okay" was said, but I don't think you believed me. See, the problem with you and me is that we have those "sad puppy dog eyes" that pretty much get us what we want. And even worse, we know how to use those bad boys. Well sure enough, you came to me with another report and asked me to help. "Nope," flew from my lips… "Wait, whoa! What do you mean no?" scrambled out of yours. "No, I'm not bailing you out this time. I have plans with Mom. We're going to lunch and then to the mall." You gave me "the look" and said the saddest "Pleeeaaseeee!" I've ever heard. I lovingly looked at you, gave you a hug and said, "Bye." You were so mad at me for leaving. You thought I was going to cave in, but I didn't. You spent the entire weekend working on your report, turned it in on Monday and hoped for the best. A couple of weeks later you received a C- as your grade, but I was very proud of you. See, that C- was yours, not mine. You learned what grades are earned on last minute work. When your next project was assigned you didn't procrastinate. I watched you work a little bit on it each day until it was due. Time and effort turned into an A-. Your A-. Pride ran through your heart that day. I was excited for you; you then knew what it felt like when your hard work is paid off. A lesson was learned. I still helped you here and there, but you never came to me with a last minute major project again (you know that I would have bailed you out if you had though).

I have to say, even though we are ten years apart in age, we've gotten along pretty well growing up. Of course there were some issues with the age difference. I was able to do things that you were nowhere near ready to do. Anytime I went out with friends you wanted to come, the phrase "Derra gets to, why can't I?" was engraved in my head. I swear that was your catch phrase for the longest time. The other phrase that was burned into my head was a favorite of Mom's. "Pick your battles." I have lost track of how many times Mom had said that to me. I think I told her one time that I didn't want to pick my battles with you. I just wanted you to stop. As you got older (and of course that meant that I got older) life ironed itself out. You had your friends and I had mine. You did your thing and I did mine. The bickering was over, well whatever it is we used to bicker over, was pretty much at an end. Now don't get me wrong, it's not like it was all rainbows and sunshine between you and I. We definitely had our moments. Like the time you flipped me off and I locked you out of the house until you apologized.

Or that time you and I had been fighting all afternoon at what turned out to be nothing really. We were just both frustrated with our own lives that we decided to take it out on each other. When Mom came home and heard us yelling at one another she put us both in my room, told us to work it out and shut the door. You and I looked at each other like, "What the hell?" An hour passed by and we both realized that we weren't really mad at each other, just mad in general so we agreed to chill out.

My favorite moment was after I had had my first eye surgery. I was watching you and Zach while Mom and Dad were out on a date night. We were all watching TV and you wanted to change the channel. I told you "No". It was Zach's turn to pick the show and that's what we were watching. You had stuck your tongue out at me and I looked at you and said, "You know that I can see you now right? The surgery worked and my vision is back." That almighty "Oh Shit" look washed over your face. "Oh yeah." was all you could come up with. I thought it was funny. Looking back on that, we can laugh at it all now. But, that's how any relationship is. Fights and arguments are bound to interrupt the peace from time to time. Even you will admit that you and I had a few good blow ups growing up, more or less during your Jr. High and high school years, which were my early twenties. Although, I felt kind of bad that there were a couple of times that we fake fought to tease Dad. You and I were (and still are) a couple of evil little genius', or are we instigators? I'm thinking it's possibly both. Hmm, oh well. The world may never know ;)

The Pop... I don't know what it is with you and the "pop" sound that the Pillsbury cans make, but even to this day you won't open one. You remember that one time when I was making rolled hot dogs for dinner and I asked you to help me out by opening the crescent rolls. You wouldn't do it. I asked you nicely, "No".

I asked a little less nicely... "No". I couldn't get it open and you refused to help. So much so that you walked to your room, packed a back pack full of books and said that you were running away. I guess you really did hate that "pop' sound. I watched you walk out the door and sit on the driveway right outside the garage. You read your books until Dad came home. After he hung up his keys he helped me with those darn crescent rolls and you walked back to your room to unpack your books. I finished making dinner and never asked you to help open any Pillsbury can again. You never had a problem eating the rolls or cinnamon rolls, but asking you to open the can was prohibited. You're such a weirdo or should I say psycho? ;)

The cleaning game... You didn't like having to clean your room as a kid. So the sneaky genius that I am, I came up with a way to trick you into cleaning your bedroom. I used to bet that you couldn't clean your room within a certain amount of time. You being a competitive chica; always took the challenge. You'd race off into your room and start cleaning it. Buzzing around like a crazy bumblebee, organizing all of your things. I would keep track of time for you and let you know how much time you had left. Each time I had you clean your room, I'd lessen the amount of time you had to clean up, gotta keep it interesting. You had a blast and I got you to do this chore without any complaints. A win-win for the both of us.

We have had a ton of awesome times too, even a few inside jokes. From the time you and I were scooping bubbles out of the dishwasher. We were out of dish detergent so I thought that adding just a touch of dish soap would do the trick. I didn't even add that much to the dishwasher, just a small amount. Who know that a smidgen of soap would turn the dishwasher into a bubble machine? Suds started spilling out the sides. I quickly turned it off and opened it up. Soo many bubbles. You and I each grabbed a cup and started scooping the suds out, dumping each cup full into the sink. In the midst of our sudsy adventure, the garage door opened up, you and I froze, looking at one another, guessing who we thought was home. Mom or Dad? Footsteps made their way towards the kitchen, then his face came around the corner. It was Dad. Whew! A ray of relief and the scooping continued. Dad just looked at us, laughed and joined the scooping gang. Mom never found out, until years later. What happens when the parents are out; stays confidential until further notice.

13 Baby! For your 13th birthday, I knew that there was only one way to celebrate… A concert! Yes, the Fall Out Boy concert that we went to was Awesome! I was so stoked when I bought the tickets, we had amazing seats. (Thank you StubHub!) I rented a limo, had souvenir money for the both of us and the night was set! The morning, however, was a topsy-turvy one. It was one of those days where all anyone can say is "This isn't happening!" You were at summer camp up in the mountains. So I printed out directions on how to get up there so Mom knew where to go. Getting up there was pretty much a piece of cake, but going back down the mountain to get back home…not so much. Mom got turned around and me being horrible with directions was absolutely no help at all. Insanity is how I can best describe picking you up from camp. After a few hours of craziness, we finally made it home. We hopped in the limo and off to Anaheim we went. But first, a stop at IN-N-Out. Because no limo ride to a concert is complete without a number 2, fries and a chocolate shake. The whole ride down we munched on our dinner and I played Fall Out Boy tunes from my iPod. And hour and 30 minutes later and there we were, The Honda Center! First stop, bathrooms. One must always check hair and makeup, plus Mother Nature was calling after all those Dr. Peppers. Second stop, souvenir stand. I believe we both bought a shirt, tote bag and a poster. Then off to our seats. Fifth row up on the left side of the stage. Our seats were perfect. DJ Paul Wall and Cobra Starship started the awesomeness off, then Plus 44 came out and rocked the house. The opening acts were amazing. Then the main reason why you, myself and thousands of other fans were there, Fall Out Boy! They popped out from under the stage and the joint was rockin'! You and I both

sang to the top of our lungs when they played Sugar We're Goin' Down. I think we got home around 1 in the morning. Best night ever. The next morning I woke up, barely having any voice. But it was totally worth it.

Summertime... Summers were always very laid back and chill. Days spent swimming in the pool, eating loads of watermelon, watching movies and of course BBQ's. You were such a "fish". You would wake up and put your swimsuit on, eat breakfast and then in the pool you went. You and Zach would swim from morning until lunch. Then you were back in the pool for a couple more hours until dinner and then after dinner you headed back to the chilly waters once again. I would lie out on the lounge chair and you'd squirt me with water from those soaker balls we had. The freezer was full of popsicles and ice pops. The fridge outside in the BBQ island was full of Snapple Peach Tea, Capri Suns and sodas. The fridge in the kitchen always had bowls of sliced watermelon, fresh cantaloupe, pineapple and bunches of green grapes. There was always a family size box of Cheez-its in the cupboard. This is pretty much what we lived off of every summer. Long days at the beach were planned. Getting up early and leaving the house by seven. Spending all day at Newport Beach. We are definitely beach babies.

Warrior Marks... so most kids learn that when one is holding a marker in their hand you use it to draw on paper and we did, most of the time. I have no idea why we did this (probably because we are 100% weird), but we would draw on each other's faces and arms. Our "warrior marks" are what we called them. At least we used Crayola Washable markers. Doodle art on our bodies, free expression baby. Lol. As we got older we would use my make-up, eyeliners and lipsticks. This was a total random thought that just popped into my head, so why not add it to the list. Sporadic mind at work ;)

The burn book... yes, the all mighty burn book. A notebook passed back and forth between you and I, pages filled with spilled out thoughts, advice shared and stresses released. Lines conjured from our minds, hearts and life in general. Questions asked and responses returned. That notebook was our safe place where we could talk about whatever we wanted to, uncensored and honest. Deep and laughable. Disclosed venting sessions, no one's feelings ever tarnished. As we ended one notebook and we began another. It was a very nostalgic feeling looking back on those dated pages of the past. A timeline of our growth in our relationship and life. Transforming from green humans to lively individuals. I still have those burn books and one day we will indulge in a day of going down memory lane and then burn those suckers...

Turn it up DJ!... hours spent downloading and creating playlist after playlist on our iPods. And depending on our current mood; different genres of guitars, drums and lyrics filled the house. You had your Big Time Rush & Hannah Montana. I had my Fall Out Boy & 3 Doors Down. Then there were bands that we both liked...Nickelback, Panic at the Disco, Destiny's Child, N'Sync...music you could shake your booty to or rock out to. On the occasion though, there were those bands that best described just how pissed off we were...

Five Finger Death Punch had a couple of slots on our "Leave me alone" playlist along with My Chemical Romance and I even think a few A Day to Remember. Yep, not one single word had to be spoken to know what kind of mood you and I were in at any given time, our playlists spoke for us.

Video game wars.... I think our favorite winter time entertainment was video games. And oh the competitions that went down in that game room. Let's see here, when we had the Dreamcast we loved that one boxing game (the name of it is currently not occupying space in my brain) and man did we ever get nuts with that. Us girls kicked the boys' butts, it was our perfected strategy of pressing every single button on that remote. Making up combinations as we duked it out with our opponents. Sometimes it pays off not knowing exactly what you're doing or how you're doing it. Then when I upgraded us to the PlayStation 2, it was the SpongeBob game, Rocket Power (that was a favorite) and those Kingdom Hearts Games. We played those until they were beat. And because we have to excel in everything we do, we searched every dark corner and hidden doors to find secret levels and characters in Kingdom Hearts. (I wonder if we have a touch of O.C.D. ;) After the PlayStation came The Wii. From Epic Mickey worlds to dance battles…tennis matches to bowling tournaments and boxing champions… Out of this world galaxies with Mario and crazy races with Yoshi. I think the Wii is our favorite toy (we do love our toys).

30 and 20 going on 5 ;)... How many weekend nights did we spend on the couch in the game room with snacks

and a Disney movie on TV. How many times did we hit the movie theater to see the latest kid movie that just debuted. Despicable Me... Madagascar... Wall-E... 25 Days of Christmas on ABC Family and of course Hocus Pocus every Halloween. Girl, you and I are going to be old ladies watching all those kid movies with our grandkids (the perfect cover up). We also like our grown up movies too, who else am I going to have Fast & Furious marathons with or text the entire movie of She's the Man, line after line (I still can't believe we did that). And lastly, the chic flicks. From The Notebook to Letters from Juliet, we do love a good romance, but you have got to stop laughing at the happy endings. I also have to stop saying that those scenarios never happen. Anyways...we do love a good movie. Just no horror movies for you, don't need you freaking out on me ;)

Graduating Class of 2012!... I was so proud of you that day. Sitting in the stands at the high school, watching you walk across the stage to receive your diploma...I couldn't believe that my baby sister was 17 and off to start her life. It seemed like it was just yesterday that you were wanting me to read you your favorite book, Barnyard Dance or laying out paper and all of the art supplies to draw (wait, I think that was yesterday, lol). And now here you were, tossing your grad cap in the air as your principal congratulates the Class of 2012. A few months later we were all at Ontario International Airport seeing you off as you boarded the plane; on your way to Lynchburg, VA. Once my five year old sister all excited for her first day of kindergarten, now 17 and off to Liberty University. I said goodbye to you in true "Derra" fashion, I stood next to you and sang "Leaving on a Jet Plane". You laughed with tear filled eyes, walked down the terminal and off you went. I am very proud of the young woman you have become. I am proud of the close relationship that you and I have. I am honored to be your sister and I know that you will accomplish amazing things in life. You my dear will always be my lollipop. <3

P.S. The ghetto Burger King will always be our place ;)

Dear Adrian,

I'm sitting here, starring at my screen, trying to figure out where to start with your letter. A nuclear bomb of thoughts exploding in my head, failing at the moment to organize themselves.

"Derra, tomorrow a friend from work is bringing her son Adrian over. He needs a little help with his math and I told Hellen you'd tutor him...."

"Ok Mom, I guess I can help him." This miniature conversation lit the spark to the beginning of a friendship that no other human could touch. I admit that as the sun rose Saturday morning my stomach was in tiny knots. Meeting new people instantly placed my body in a twisted shy mode, especially if those newbies were boys. I guess being "different" does a little more damage than we want to pay attention to. "Ding" rang the doorbell and the words "They're here" fell from my Mom's mouth. You and your Mom walked through the door and for the split second that I looked up, I noticed that you looked as nervous as I did. Awkwardly sitting at the table, I started perusing the section of math you were on and shifted gears from shy mode to tutor mode. The ball rolled with fractions and quickly snowballed into school, friends, movies, music and everything else in our young lives. Before we knew it your Mom was back to pick you up. A day that woke up twisting my nervous system ended with a sunset dipped in neon.

Every time I somehow catch Six Days and Seven Nights on TV, I think of you. Most friends have a song, but as we both know, you and I are not most people (not sure if that's a good or bad thing yet). Saturday night, the dollar theater was bursting at the seams with fellow teeny boppers. You, Andrew, myself and a friend of mine hopped out of my Ma's van, purchased tickets and found the last few available seats in a swarm of chatter. Memory loss has consumed certain sections of that night, maybe it's because my brain is overcrowded. I just remember you and I sitting next to each other, sharing a bag of popcorn and predicting how certain situations were going to pan out in the movie.

Confession time, remember when you asked me to your ROTC Christmas Dance? I do, and not for the reasons I should. I was weirdly nervous about that night. For whatever reason there were Amazonian sized butterflies taking residence in my stomach. Your Mom dropped us off at your school and as we entered the gym, my nervousness started to melt away. None of the kids I went to school with were there, the only person I knew was you. No one from my territory could interfere... or so I thought. While you went to check out what kind of food they were serving at the buffet they set up, a girl from my side of the tracks came over to the table I was sitting at. This girl and I did not get along, not even the tiniest bit. I won't go into all the dirty details of what she said to make me do what I did next because I believe that some things need to stay buried. As little Miss Prissy left, you came back and I told you that I wasn't feeling very well. I had you call your Mom to come get us... I lied my ass off, my pants should have produced flames. I didn't want you caught in the middle of my war with my enemy. Her problem was with me, and if there was one thing that butthead was good at it was spreading believable rumors. I couldn't care less if she wanted to mess with me, but I wasn't about to let her mess with you. I have always felt like I ruined that night and I am truly sorry for that. I am sorry that we never got to dance.

Time passing... Our lives completely separate yet spiraling downward into darkness at the same time. The next time we saw each other was when you, your Mom and Andrew came over to go to Saturday night church with us. Both of us appearing to be the same on the outside while a hint of differences gleamed out from within. I was pissed at the world as my light was dimming more and more with each passing minute. I tried like hell that night to smile and fake happiness, but I think you knew that I was off. Faking life around you wasn't easy. I'm able to let my guard down and be real with you (I love/hate that about you ;))

A few years had arrived and departed. I had been going through with what seemed like an endless battle with my demons. You had been going down the alley ways of your own hell. Neither one of us able to be accessible for anyone, let alone each other.

I remember the night that I was messing around with the creations of playlists on my laptop; a tiny icon appeared in the top right corner stating that I had a new message in my Myspace inbox. It was from a mutual friend who gave me your Mom's cell number. The curious George in me texted her to see what's up. Hellen texted back giving me your house number and said to give you a call. It was around nine o'clock and you answered in a tired voice. I had forgotten that you're not the biggest night owl in the world. You are that oh so annoying morning person who's perky and ready to start the day at 6 am... you people baffle me ;) We talked for hours... I gave up the inside scoop on how I got my first book published, you read me a few pieces of your work and then we just discussed life. Even though we hadn't spoken or seen each other in a few years, talking on the phone that night... it was like we just saw each other last week. I have always admired that about our crazy friendship. No matter the distance (distance or time) we just pick right back up where we leave off. No one hurt that too much time has passed, just two friends either shooting the bull or indulging in deep thoughts. That winter and spring we hung out all the time. My house, the mall (Barnes and Nobles then Panda Express). And the movies.

That weekend that you spent at my house was one of my favorite memories. You, Lu and I sat around the BBQ island playing cards, munchin' on pretzels, enjoying a refreshing bud light lime (you added a pinch of salt to the beers before we drank them... made them soooo much better) and just enjoyed the evening and each other's company. Me being the lightweight that I was, had a small buzz after one beer. I don't remember what time we all ended up crashing, but I do remember it was a great night. The next day we all just hung at the house watching movies and cooking up some good eats.

Summer hit and life spun into crazy mode again. I started writing again and dealing with certain family issues. You started school, met a girl and had your own family issues you were dealing with. Even though we didn't hang out as much, we still kept in contact via phone and Facebook (Myspace became outdated, it was so last season).

Remember that time that I said the "L" word... yeah, I know. You were the first guy I had ever said that to. I debated back and forth forever on whether or not I should tell you how I felt. Having the blind courage to say that you love someone is terrifying all on its own, but when it's the person who you've known since Jr. high, its flat out "scare the shit out of me" terrifying. There is a gate that lies in the center of a friendship. On the left side lies the world where all is copasetic. You hang out, have those stupid moments, deep conversations and know that no matter what life throws at you, there is that one person who knows you, listens with an open ear and non- judgmental heart. On the right side lies the unknown. The place where the "what ifs" live. If your feelings start to move stronger towards the 'more than just friends' range, things start to get sticky. If you don't say anything then nothing will change and you'll just bury those other feelings. Which in its stupidity sounds pretty solid, except when unexpected variables start showing up in your brilliant equation. On the other hand, you could swallow your anxiety and have the guts to tell them how you feel. Here three different scenarios pop up on the menu. Firstly, they could reply with the "I love you" back and the new journey of transitioning from "just friends" to "more" begins. And if all is driven down the "perfectly imperfect" route you may just have that "happily ever after" most people are searching for. Secondly, the feelings are still mutual and you try out the outfits of "a couple", but somehow the inevitable happens and the relationship doesn't work out. Hearts are broken. At this point there is also as huge possibility that not only do you no longer have that certain someone special in your life, but you no longer have your best friend either. One stone... two big blows to your world. Then lastly there's the good old third scenario. The "I love you" bomb is dropped, however the feeling isn't reciprocated on their end. At this point either you both find a way to fly past the awkwardness and remain friends or for reasons only you know, the friendship ends. Scenario one is a rarity, a fairy-tale we all secretly dream about, but rare none the less... scenario two and three have the highest percentage rate in the final outcome when opening the latch on the gate and crossing over. For us, it was scenario three. You broke my heart as carefully as you could and I unburied my box, placed my embarrassment inside and reburied it six feet under. A couple of weeks passed and I played it as though I had never opened that gate. We are, if nothing else, resilient. It took me a while and a few casual relationships to get over it all, but I came to the conclusion that you were right. You and I as friends was the best place for us.

8 months...the period of time that we allowed to be wasted due to white noise that slipped from drunken

keys. A conversation online that started out as an invitation to a BBQ and ended with a deletion. Looking back on that day, I realize that you and I didn't speak for almost a year due to both us having synchronized stupidity moments. I invited you over to hang, knowing that you'd decline because your girlfriend didn't like me and instead of just keeping my thoughts locked inside my head I typed them out for your eyes to read. You took my words and tweaked meaning that was invisible into them. Replies typed, wrongs being read and then ...done. I had pissed you off and I knew it. You misread my words and I think you knew it. The second I slammed my laptop down the recognition of my stupid moment downloaded into my mind and I knew that the only cure for the brokenness that was just born would be an apology. But, that was nowhere near the top of either one of our to-do lists. You deleted me and I deleted you. Not a single day passed where I didn't kick myself for pressing the destruction button. Days spun into months. I texted your Mom and asked her to wish you a Happy Birthday for me when the September breeze rolled in. I couldn't even just swallow my pride, apologize and text you that myself. A couple of months later my phone vibrated with the notification from Facebook. "I'm Sorry..." along with further explanation glowed on my screen. "I'm Sorry too..." was sent back to your screen. And just like that, stitches mended our wastefulness and neither one of us ever looked back. It's crazy how typed words can create instant insanity. Our eyes soak in what's on our screens, then our minds insert tone, giving these innocent words life of either goodness or evilness. Sometimes evil wins...not forever, but it definitely burrows itself and leaves its mark.

You may not realize, but you have been one of the biggest impacts in my life. You never judged me, you never felt pity towards me and you never treated me differently because of my EB. You taught me what true friendship meant and what it means to have ones back. To never judge based on the outside cover and most importantly... The only approval you need in life is your own. I could confide anything with you and know that it wasn't going to be next day's gossip. You and I are different yet the same in a variety of aspects. And I want you to know that you're not just a friend, you're family. I love you man! ;) No matter where life may take us, no matter the distance driven between us, I am always here for you...No matter what. Just light up that Bat signal in the night sky...I'll be there.

funny, you're the broken one, but i'm the only one who needed saving, 'cause when you never see the light it's hard to know which one of us is caving.

Dear Daddy,

From Batman to The Avengers... From the NY Giants to the LA Kings... from Journey to 3 Doors Down... from Die Hard to Silence of the Lambs... and from Oreo's to Reese's... I have you to thank for molding me into the biggest superhero lover, sports fan, sweet toothed, movie and music maniac nerd that I am today. You and I have had quite the journey together. Adventures with Dad and a lot of them.

I used to love when we lived down in Glendora and anytime I went with you to run errands, you would jump the train tracks that we'd often come across, in that little silver Toyota truck of yours. As the tracks came into view you would "press the petal to the metal" and gun it. Air was caught and it was frickin' awesome! Except the time I thought Ma' would like it, just as much as we did, but she did not. We tried making her apart of our "jump the tracks" adventures, but turns out it was strictly a Dad and Derra thing. Moms are not allowed.

I also remember when you and I would wrestle around in the living room. I'd jump on you like I was some badass WWE wrestler and we'd tussle back and forth. Although, come to think of it, Ma wasn't too happy about this either. Hmmm, I don't why. I loved it.

Remember the time you allowed me the privilege to style your hair. I thought I did a phenomenal job for only being five years young. I had placed so many colorful clips and bows in your hair. You looked like a magical rainbow unicorn, stylin' Sir. I don't know why you wouldn't let Ma' take a few snap shots, you looked fabulous! Who knows, maybe a modeling agency would have signed you for how amazing you rocked that sparkling hairdo and you could've become a famous model for CK. ;)

I do have to confess something, as much as this pains me, I purposely asked you to play games with me while you were watching the Kings play or any other game for that matter. I knew you would only pay half attention to what we were playing and that I could beat you, every time. Yes, my evil genius brain was already in effect at the age of six. My bad. Perhaps I watched one too many Pinky and The Brain cartoons on Saturday mornings. Picked up a few tips from Brain.

Some of my most favorite memories are when we would go camping in the desert with Uncle Ricky and Graham. You guys would go dirt bike riding and I'd hang with Ma'. Campfires at night, Graham riding around the fire on a mini bike singing his jam. Then there was the infamous "Night of the Scorpions" …lol. I don't even know how many times that story is told when we get together with my favorite goonie (Graham). I still have a stack of old photos from our desert adventures. I love the pics were the skies are clouded in a gloomy grayness, which I know were your favorite days to go riding. Hmmm, do you think there's some connection here as to why I love a good gloom and doom skied day or is it just a happy coincidence?

Hershey Park Madness... You always had my back Dad. You never let anyone tell me that I couldn't do something. I remember that time when we were at Hershey Park and I wanted to go on the Whirl Around ride. You sit in the bucket seats and spin in all directions. Somewhat similar to the Tea Cups at Disneyland. However, when we got to the front of the line the ticket taker person wouldn't allow me to go on. Not because I wasn't old enough or because I wasn't at the appropriate height, but because he saw my hands and figured that I couldn't go on due to my "Handicappism". I was so upset, I started walking towards Mom in tears when you caught up to me, picked me up and walked back over to the ride. "I thought that I couldn't go on it Dad." You looked into my saddened eyes and said, "You want to go on this ride, then you're going on it." You explained to the ticket guy that there was no reason why I couldn't go on the ride. He looked at you, took our tickets and let us on. You, myself and Tom's nephew sat in the bucket, and spun around and around. It was the best ride ever (well I was only 10, so a lot of things were the best ever). I remember that memory as though it was yesterday. Not because of the ride or because Tom's nephew almost threw up on you, but because you stood up for me. You showed me first hand that I shouldn't let anyone stop me from doing what I want to do.

Video game monster... ahh... There's nothing like the classics. Like the original Nintendo. Weekends spent assisting a little Italian plumber defeat a spiky dragon king and rescue a peachy princess. From worlds of Gratius to MotoCross, virtual hours were gamed. As technology progressed so did our gaming systems, upgrading from the classic Nintendo to Super Nintendo, were new worlds were ventured. Zelda fought his enemies in search of the Tri-Force and Donkey Kong protected his plush banana jungle. When the Dreamcast from Sega made its premiere then we became certified Crazy Taxi Drivers, raced through the magical world of Disneyworld and collected gold rings in Sonic's world. Sadly the Dreamcast came and went like a cherry blossom. PlayStation 2 whirled its way into the games room where battles were fought and villains destroyed in Kingdom's Heart. Nintendo joined the family once again when the Wii was born. Boxing matches sucker punched out, bowling tournaments pinned down, Halo Shells launched at fellow racers in Mario's world of GoKarts, Epic adventures spun with Mickey, football players scoring touchdown after touchdown in a Madden and many a dance battles had, because sometimes one needs to Just Dance!

Fishing... Clear blue skies that day. Poles, tackle box and snacks all packed in the car and off we went to Hesperia Lakes. I had never been fishing before, but I was a tiny ball of excitement and determined to catch my first fish. Car parked, the perfect spot selected, chairs set up and now it was time to learn how to bate my hook and catch one of these lake creatures. You showed me what bate to choose based on what type of fish were in the lake and how to place it on the hook. Since we were fishing for trout you placed a small brightly colored green ball at the end of my hook and then it was time to cast off. With my Donald Duck fishing pole in hand, I swung it back and then flung it forward, watching as the line traveled further away from me. "Plop" went the hook as it sank into the rippling blue liquid. The next step seemed long, sitting and waiting until an unsuspecting fish bit the bate. However, we talked about school, friends, and how we were going to cook all the delicious fish we were going to catch; the time seemed to pass by somewhat fast. Tugging at my pole, I started to freak out a bit. Some fish was trying to steal my pole.

"Give him a little slack... You don't want him to get away."

"Ok Dad, like this?'

"Good girl, just like that. Great job kiddo!" and there it was in all its rainbow scaly glory. I had caught my first fish. Quite an epic moment in my 8th year of living on earth. The park ranger even awarded me with a certificate, "Derra Sabo Has Caught Her First Rainbow Trout Here at Hesperia Lakes" ...Yes, I admit; my girly ego was about the same size of my little body at that moment. I knew what I was talking about to all my friends at school come Monday. There was only one task left to do before packing everything back up… gut and clean our freshly caught friends. Now I didn't take part in this, but I watched. Oh man! What a scene. Knife in hand, you slit a straight even gash in each fish's stomach and cleaned out all the red gooey grossness. One of the pleasures of living a kid's life, your dinner comes already cooked and tasty looking on the plate. All we do is chow down. That day I learned the cycle of that poor fish's life, although, the gross factor didn't last too long, because once we were home and you grilled up all the trout on the BBQ. I was ready to eat it. It smelled so good and looked delicious. I ate the whole fish.

Casted for the next eight weeks... Downfall to having EB (well at least one of them) anytime I had hand surgery I was sentenced to wear these uncomfortable casts for the next two months while the doctors tried to fix a broken part of me. Somehow, and I still don't know how, you made life in plaster fun. When I was four and had both arms casted, you told me that I was like Robo Cop. You stood behind me, placed your hands under each heavy cast and started making shooting sounds while turning my arms from side to side. I was shooting all the bad guys. Protecting you and Mom from all the evil villains in the house.

Four years later and round two of the casted life. However, the upside this time around was that I would only have one hand in a cast at a time. You drew all over my cast so that it would look cool. At the time you worked for Terminex and since you were the "Bug Guy", that's what you doodled. Different bugs all over my right hand and lower arm. Helping me stay fashionable as always (you did buy me my first pair of pink Nikes. stylin' from the get-go). And being the kind Dad that you are, you did leave a little room for my friends at school to fill in the blanks with their artwork.

Oh, that leads me to the times that you would surprise me at school on random occasions with lunch. You would bring me a happy meal from McDonalds and whatever meal you'd ordered for yourself. You would eat with my friends and I in the cafeteria. You would always order extra fries and share them around the table. "Ok small people, you can eat all the fries you want, just don't touch my burger." I certainly did have the "Cool Dad". I think that was one of my favorite memories as a munchkin.

Music Mania... The year I turned seven, you and Ma (or should I say Santa) gave me a purple boom box for Christmas. My first boom box. I could now grab my Barbie microphone and rock out in my room to all my New Kids on the Block tapes. I didn't have any CD's yet, but I figured that I'd buy some with my allowance. One night, when you arrived home from work, you came into my room with your hands behind your back and told me that you had a surprise for me. I closed my eyes as instructed and then you said the words "Ok, open".

There it was; a thin square case that read, "No Doubt". I couldn't believe it. I placed that prismatic CD in my boom box and listened to the sweet sounds of "Spiderwebs", "I'm Just a Girl" and "Don't Speak". Tragic Kingdom vibrated my room every day for I don't even remember how long. You bought me my first CD and kick started a love for bands like 3 doors Down, Journey, Green Day, Blink 182, U2 and so many more. I was an official lover of music.

Hello Clarice… as a last gift on my 12th birthday, you had convinced Ma to allow me to stay up and watch Silence of the Lambs with you. I was stoked! Staying up past nine and I was about to watch my first creepy movie. A huge bowl of popcorn was popped and seats were dibbed. I'll never forget how intensely I viewed this mind twisting film. Eyes glued to the glowing screen and ears pumping in Anthony Hopkin's amazingly psychotic performance. I think your evil little plan was to scare the crap out of me, but haha sucker. Your plan was blown to pieces because not only did I love that movie, I became intrigued with horror movies. Creepy, weird and scare your pants off movies became a love of mine. TV shows as well. I'm a total fan of Criminal Minds, Stalker and American Horror Story. Life's no fun without a good scare… right?! ;) This also makes me remember the time that you and I watched Texas Chainsaw Massacre. I had already finished my school day (senior year was a breeze) and you happened to have the afternoon off. Since Ma was at work and the kids were in school, you and I thought we'd pop in a delightful afternoon movie. From the very beginning you were totally grossed out. I guess watching a girl blow out her brains with a gun and watching them splatter all over the back windshield of a car isn't your forte. I just sat there completely into the movie, eating a roast beef sandwich. Nothing says Happy Friday like some people being cut into pieces by a psycho carrying a chainsaw, terrifying screams vibrating the walls (the power of a kickass surround sound system) and a delicious snack. 'Twas perfect...at least I thought it was.

Double Dare... It was my thirteenth birthday; the plan was set. Dinner at my choice of restaurant and then a movie of my choice. I made myself all pretty and off we (you, Ma and myself) went. I had decided on The Olive Garden for dinner (those breadsticks are addictive!) Before we drove to the restaurant, Ma had you stop at Wal-Mart. You two led me to the jewelry department. At first I wasn't sure why we there, but then I saw it. The Winnie the Pooh watch I had been wanting. The band was light brown leather with honey bees burned into it. Pooh bear was in the center of the watch's face and the second hand was five honey bees that buzzed around him. It was the cutest watch. As you were purchasing my surprise gift I noticed a sign that said... "We Pierce Ears". I looked at you with my evil genius face, "Hey Dad... I double dare you to get your ear pierced." Now being the little Miss Smarty pants that I was, I knew what your answer was going to be. Or at least I thought I did. You totally shocked me when you turned to the employee and said, "And I'll take one stud in my left ear please." Jaw dropped, I turned to Ma... "Is he really going to do it?" All Ma could say was, "I think so..." And sure enough you did. Before I knew it, one of your earlobes had a tiny sparkle shimmering from it. I now know where my Dare disease comes from. ☺ After our Wal-Mart adventure, we headed off to eat and then caught Phenomenon at the theater. It was an awesome b-day!

Apple Cinnamon Pancakes... I love when you make your pancakes for breakfast (even to this day). As a kid waking up on a Saturday morning to the smell of cinnamon swirling its way into my bedroom. I knew that there were some good eats being cooked up in the kitchen. I'd pop out of bed, get dressed and get to the kitchen to watch you make the last batch of those oh so fluffy pancakes. Piping hot, you would stack three on a plate for me. I'd smear them with butter, drizzle them with sticky maple syrup and sink my teeth into all the appley goodness

Grilled peanut butter sandwiches were your other specialty that I loved. Crunchy and buttery on the outside, ooey-gooey peanuty on the inside. Heaven in toasted sandwich form. And don't worry. I have forgiven you for that whole spaghetti, hot dog and rice incident. We won't speak of it again, it's in the past... lol. I know you worked a lot when I was growing up, so when you were home and made everyone breakfast, it just turned into a tasty memory to add to the box. It made those days all the more special and delicious.

From bedtime stories to Saturday morning cartoons, I loved being the only kid in the joint and having my d-a-d-d-y all to myself. When Alyssa and Zachery were born, I thought that our adventures would be over, but they weren't. In fact, I think that the "adventures with Dad' became even more adventurous with more munchkins creating chaos in the house. Triple the fun!

Like that time Ma' was away for the dental convention in Anaheim. It was just one Dad and his three crazy kids, home alone, all weekend long. No maternal supervision. A trip to Wal-Mart was made and four water guns were purchased. The battle was already brewing before we got home with our new weaponry. Teams picked, all the sinks and hoses on the premises became reloading stations and water tanks filled. War running through our veins… it was on! And since Ma' wasn't home that meant it was "no holds barred" … All senses on alert for enemies and wild animals that roamed the grounds (two labs named shadow and crash along with our cat named boots… very vicious). Icy cold water shot through the air pinning its intended target (mainly because Alyssa and I put ice cubes in our water tanks before filling them with water). It was two days of shivering amusement, until Ma' arrived home on Sunday and saw her kids sliding down the hallways soaked from head to toe. I still feel kinda bad that when she asked who bought us the guns and allowed us to have a water gun fight in the house, each one of us kids turned and pointed our fingers towards you. What can I say, all's fair in love and water wars.

Motorhome madness… those two words are pretty self- explanatory. From camping at Ventura Beach to backyard poker games. We all had a blast in that motorhome. Remember the time that all of us kids went with you to gas it up and as we turned the corner the back door flung open. I was sitting in the chair that was right next to it (quite a refreshing breeze once the door flung open). "Ummm Dad…the doors open." You looked back and just started cracking up. No pulling over to the side of the road so one of us could close it, there was no need because as soon as you turned another corner it slammed shut. Alyssa pulled the door handle towards her as I locked the deadbolt to it. "Did you girls get it all locked up? Are you all good back there?" And of course Lu and I responded as we always do. "Of course Dad! We got it all under control!"

Washing that bad boy was an adventure in itself. Us girls always chose to make the inside all spic n' span while you two boys washed the outside. Cleaning the inside was a picnic compared the outside. Your girls definitely knew all the ways to cheat the system ;)

Even when the motorhome was stationary good times were had. Summer night poker games! Deck of cards shuffled and dealt. Everyone dished out their chips (in this case it was more like Oreos, skittles and liquorice…kid style poker). Round after round, hand after hand… big hands won, bluffs made and sugar rushed pots won (and eaten).

We only had that big rolling turd for a few years, but it held within it some of the more infamous moments engraved in my memory. I was a bit bummed when you and Ma' sold it, but I know that as we all grew older and became more and more involved in our own lives that the poor motorhome just sat behind the RV gate. It needed a new home.

The Darkness Falls… I'm not sure if you will remember this, but when I was losing my vision, there was a moment during that darkness when you made me feel less like a broken mess. Our house on Cuyamaca

Rd. was in the process of being built and there was one evening in particular that we went to go see the progress of it. I was sitting on the window pane in what was going to be my room, trying to visualize what it looked like then and how it would look after all of my things were moved in (visualizing was pretty much how I saw my world those days). You came in, sat next to me and asked if I was alright. I of course lied my ass off and replied, "Yeah, I'm fine." Instead of trying to talk me into spilling my guts out as to how I was actually doing or what was going on my head, you simply said that you know a little bit of how I'm feeling and explained why. You told me that there was a time in your younger life when you had a hard time seeing and how it made life a touch more difficult. The world came into view after your surgery. You told me that I was a strong girl and asked me to promise that I wouldn't lose hope...in anything. I never thanked you for that moment. Thank you Dad <3

Many adventures lived... many moments created and stored... Life changing fast and furiously, but no matter how chaotic, no matter how frustrating, no matter how dark... your ears were wide open when I needed to vent. As my world grew dark, your shoulder soaked up my tears. When my heart broke into pieces, your arms held the rest of me together.

A solid sense of work ethic... not sweating the small stuff... Not putting off what I could do today until tomorrow... these are some of life's downloads that are hardwired into my DNA. Lessons you taught me. Lessons that weren't just discussed, but put into action every day. I witnessed how you implemented those wise expressions into your own world. You worked a lot, but it was to provide for your family. I never went without. I never had a need or even a want that wasn't fulfilled. I will be the first to tell anyone that I was a spoiled kid, but not in a rotten way. Chores were done and allowance was earned. As I grew older I learned that there are times in life when you help out family and friends with no sense of a return. A helping hand that has no dollar sign attached to it is the best way to learn humility and humbleness (which are the best kind of vibes to have flowing through your system)

Dear Past Me,

Hey kid, what's up? So I'm here to relay a message to you from the future us. I know, that is totally insane, but just entertain this letter for a moment or two. You my dear are going to be born with a label attached to you. Not literally, in a metaphoric sense. We are all born different, however you are being born into a world that believes in what is known as "Normalcy". There are those who believe that being normal and having a normal life is what is socially acceptable. The word "different" raises a sense of fear and questionability. Thoughts of "There must be something wrong with them" tend to be the main topic with those who think of themselves as normal. You will live a life as an outcast, always looking in. The wallflower and the late bloomer. Those who don't understand will try to fix you because in their eyes you are broken. You will be blindly judged and pitied. There will be those who will make fun of you and try to tear you down simply because they're mean spirited. They get pleasure out of making the different ones feel like freaks.

As you grow older in age and start new adventures you will meet people from all different walks of life. You will quickly learn that some of these people you will find similarities and common ground with, some you will have unbreakable friendships with, some will become your nemeses and some you just won't like. The same goes for all. We all have family, we all have friends, we all have acquaintances, we all have enemies and we all have those who we just don't care for, but still have a sense of common courtesy when around them.

Your childhood is awesome! Loving parents who you will have countless adventures with. Memories made at baseball games, hockey games, trips to Disneyland, vacations and so much more. You will be grounded once in a while, but that's just because you won't always keep your mouth shut when you should (doesn't always pan out being a bit of a smartass). You will acquire a love for the arts, get lost in the soul that is spoken through music and develop a taste for creating delicious bites in the kitchen. Bookworm syndrome will be an illness that's incurable and you will become a special-forces agent in the world of words. Being the oldest of three will create plenty of chaotic adventures. You'll love it though and it turns out that you're pretty good at being a sister. You, Alyssa and Zach will get into plenty of trouble together and have tons of awesome memories. Yep, you're going to have an awesome childhood. The only downfall to this era of your young years, besides the whole EB situation, are the nightmares that will enter your wonderful slumbering hours. They're pretty frickin' scary to start out with, but then in a very weird way you'll become used to them. So used to them in fact that they almost become a part of your life. It's like these insane mini "zzzz" thieves make up a part of who you'll become. Look, I never said it would all make sense, I'm just trying to help a girl out.

Elementary school and Jr. High will have its ups and downs, but great experiences will fill your photo box. You will meet some very kind and funny kids that you will build awesome friendships with. School is a safe place for you. Learning all subjects from History to Math, English and Science, Cooking and Computer Technology… Your brain will soak in an abundance of knowledge. High school on the other hand will become a bit like a roller coaster ride. You will encounter kids that will try to break you and kick you while you're down simply because they find some disgusting enjoyment out of it. How you view the world and the humans living in it will change drastically. Positions from being in the "it" crowd of laughter and coolness will switch to becoming the freak who is banished to looking on the inside from your out casted home. Your heart will be broken by one single word that will change the way you look at yourself in the mirror. Becoming labeled as "damaged" is going to cause some major confusion in your fragile mind. And to top this tainted sundae off is a blinded cherry. Yes, as much as it pains me to add to the depression that will engulf your world, darkness will follow. Due to circumstances beyond your control, your vision will become clouded and rapidly fade with each stormy day. You my dear; are going to encounter some major tests during your high school years. Bending and twisting along the way. Fighting with every ounce of your soul as you fight to grasp onto the candle light. Trust me though, you will survive all of this, I know it sounds as though I'm mocking you by saying that, but it's one hundred percent titanium. However, fair warning, you will actually end up not just at your breaking point, but you will actually break. Before you can heal from these four years, you must first put back together the 1,000 piece puzzle that is your heart. That moment of hitting rock bottom will arrive and you will try to end your fragile life. You will feel as though your life is nothing more than a heavy damaged burden on your family and that the point of existence is moot. That shiny invitation into heaven will feel so calming in your hands. A tiny slice of redness will deliver a sense of peace. Then a droplet of your spirit will flash a glimpse of why you cannot yet leave this world. A defining journey of rebuilding will present itself.

I say all of this to you not because I want you to try and stop these moments from happening, but to prepare you. To prepare you for the brokenness you'll feel and for the stitching that will follow. The day will come...the cry for help will be answered...the knife will drop and God will save you. None of what's to come can be altered or differed from, or a chain reaction will occur that will forever change the person you're destined to become.

The tiny flickering candle at the end of the tunnel will grow into a warming and comforting fireplace with each step you crawl forward. The days of darkness and sorrow will become unstuck, vibrant technicolors will swim back into your line of sight. Your family and best friend will assist you in the reconstruction of "you". Your life will start to take shape and you will slowly start to blossom. Yes, you are a late bloomer to the starting line, but once your soul is filled with the supply that it needs, life will begin.

Let's talk about the "twenties" era. I'm going to be blunt with you, your twenties are going to be weird and suck all at the same time. Not to any extent where you can't handle things or feel as though you're going to break again, but awkwardness will move in for a while.

So, in case you hadn't already noticed, boys aren't the biggest factor in high school for you, too many crap storms taking over. Guys start to enter the picture later on. You will meet a few interesting dudes. New experiences with how guys act and what they're really after will become clearer in the crystal ball. Between 21 and 26 you will meet and have some, ummmm, interesting relationships. No wait, I thought of a better word...Crazy. That's it! You will definitely have some crazy relationships. Firsts as well. A lot of firsts. From that first kiss to losing your "V" card. Your first fight which will lead to your first break up and yes, your first broken heart. And consequently, your first rebound relationship. Sometimes the "no strings attached" is a better alternative. The whole concept of love doesn't really make an appearance during all this craziness. Not to say that you won't know what actual love for another person feels or looks like. You will, it's just not with any of these guys. The love you will have towards another will be the best unknown love that will hold a place in your heart forever. Now at this point, none of your relationships will have the "serious" factor. More casual than anything, dipping your toes in the water before jumping in. Then you will meet a guy that you think is your "happily ever after", but will soon realize that he is just a pile of lying and cheating bullshit that's covered by smoke and mirrors. You won't see any of it at first because the glitter of love will blind you, but as the lies start to creep to the surface and the others start to peek from around the Myspace corner, the beer goggles will drop and soberness will kick in. His temper will be unveiled when you place him in the corner of honesty and call him out on all the bull. A moment of weakness will offer itself up, but surprisingly it will be declined. A sense of strength and courage that you didn't even know existed will fight back. And another first will be added to the list. The first time you were the heartbreaker and not the heartbroken. He will test you after he's gone, calls and texts will invade your phone, threats will be dished out and his stalking skills brought to light. There will be one downfall to his obsessive plan...You. Thoughts of being able to control you like a puppet will fill his puppeteering head. But, you will cut those strings so quickly, his head will spin. Turns out that you are definitely not a chica that will allow herself to be played. Also, turns out that those years of being an out-cast will actually come in handy. Makes it simpler when learning how to play the game and how others play it. Don't hate the player, hate the game. The end result of all of this will affect you in ways you never thought, the tiny pebble that is your ex-boyfriend will ripple the world of love. First ripple: encase your heart in a steel chest with a gold lock and ditch the key in a safe place. Second ripple: build walls surrounding the chest. Third ripple: trust is on the lowest level and will not easily be regained. Fourth ripple: question the integrity of what love really is and if it's worth the risk. It's tough to come back from being duped. In the end, you'll be more upset with yourself than him, even though you weren't the screw up.

After all that is said and done, you will decide to take a break from the world of love, which is going to be a good thing. Time to repair is much needed. And besides, there's going to be some health issues that you'll need to concentrate on. And they're going to need your full attention. So, as you know you're a twig. Living life with EB means that your metabolism is high and gaining weight is more of a task than you'd think. You don't weigh much to begin with and unfortunately it's going to take a toll on your body. You won't eat the way you should and the proof will be in the fact that you will start to malfunction. Loss of weight which will lead to a skin and bones fright. This will trickle down into becoming bed ridden, sick with bronchitis for almost four months. Weakness, dizziness, loss of appetite, huge loss of sleep, constant coughing and pains felt from within. Headaches resulting from dehydration will pound your brain constantly, breathing will become painful, numbness will run down your arm and your heart will attack you in a very painful way. It will feel as though the Grimm Reaper is knocking at your door. A two year journey to becoming healthy on the inside and out will be embarked upon. Doctors' appointments will fill your calendar, blood will be drawn and tested and the news will be delivered. The final step to begin your recovery, the call. Yep, that call at 11:00 at night telling you to go the emergency room right away. Girl, guess why. Hold on a sec... you should sit down for this. Ok...your haemoglobin (iron) level is so low that you will literally stun your doctors at the fact that your, well, basically not dead. The fact that you're still walking around and breathing instead of on your death bed is a miracle in itself. Changes need to be implemented and they need to be implemented immediately. And yes, you will become white as a ghost and freak out when you're told that if your health doesn't improve, you could go into cardiac arrest at any moment.

Now we come to the fork in the road. On the left you will encounter a life of monthly injections, blood transfusions every few months and constant trips to the blood bank so the vampires can take all of your blood. On the right you will encounter a change in diet, a daily vitamin, blood tests and check-ups every few months until your levels are out of the death zone. Take a guess which highway you're going to choose to cruise down. The word "Duh" comes to mind. A weekend filled with research on iron enriched foods, the best vitamins to take and what foods also help your body to absorb the iron will be a weekend well spent. And even though it may look like nothing but impossibilities, in just a few months you will be the healthiest you've ever been. Iron levels will rise, a few healthy pounds will be packed onto your teeny tiny body and all your aches and pains will dissipate into nothing. You will glow from the inside out. I know this is going to sound batty, but your life is going to begin when you hit 30. You're going to be Ok chica!

Dear Bubba,

OMG! Here we go... I know that you'll agree with me when I say that you and I have been through a lot together! Plenty of chaos and craziness created by the two of us. When you were born I was so excited to have a little brother. I was now a big sister who had two siblings, one of each. Lol. I gotta be honest with you though, you were a very grumpy baby Dude. You cried a lot. On the upside, you calmed down as you grew into your toddler years. You were pretty funny running around in your flannel shirts with jeans and your little hiking boots. You looked like the Brawny paper towel guy, in miniature size. That was your favorite outfit to wear, and that's when I came up with your nickname...Bubba. On the weekends you would always ask me to style your hair for you. As I played hairdresser, you'd stand on your tippy toes so that you could see your reflection in the mirror, just barely. You were the kid who had to have his room clean and everything had a certain spot that it belonged. I think you were the most organized 3 year old I knew.

Houston, we have a problem...you were a chatty little dude, the only downfall was that you weren't speaking English. Gibberish was your native tongue for a few months. Everyone had a hard time understanding what you would ask for, but for some odd reason, I knew exactly what you were saying. Don't ask me why because I never took gibberish. Since I could understand your language, Ma' deemed me your translator. Anytime you would ask her or Dad for something, they would look at me and say, "what did he ask for?' It's a good thing though; at least someone in the house could break the language barrier.

Morning tours... Remember our morning walks to school? I loved those; it was a 15 minute walk from our house, the perfect amount of time for us to chat about whatever you wanted. You, Alyssa and I would discuss what you had going on in school, friends and any topic that would pop into you guys' heads. If it had rained, I would always turn our walks into tours. I would point out the different puddles and explain how they were mini lakes. Each had a crazy made up name and of course the one rule during the tour was, "Please no fishing in the lakes and ponds." I enjoyed our walks to and from school. Except during the winter and that's only because you never wanted to wear a jacket. I had a 6 year old brother trying to act like some tough dude who didn't need a stinkin' jacket. I would let you go because the argument at 8 am wasn't worth it. Halfway to school you would always ask me to hold you because you were freezing your stubborn toosh off. "No way man, you're too heavy. I guess that jacket's looking pretty sweet right now isn't it?" But, after a few trips in the chilly air, you grabbed a jacket. Lesson learned, problem solved.

All Hallows' Eve... Halloween, yours and my favorite time of the year. 24 hours of ghostly spirits wandering the skies. 24 hours were all monsters, from all walks of life, are gruesomely accepted. 24 hours of creepy bliss. Every year I would take you trick-or-treating around our neighborhood. You would dress up like some weird grim reaper guy or like that ghoulish white masked dude from 'Scream". Around 7pm we would venture out into the haunted night. Flashlight in hand, I would watch as you house hopped, filling your bag full of fun sized candy bars. One hour was all it took for you to collect a 6 month supply of chocolatey goodness. Once we arrived back home I would collect my payment for my services as your body guard. 4 Reese's peanut butter cups and two snickers. The rest of the stash was yours and it was well earned. It's funny how after all of the good candy was devoured, left at the bottom of the bowl was always the crappy fruity candy that seemed like it was ten years' stale. Trash can candy is what I call it. It's also funny how every one of us kids would organize our Halloween candy based on its quality. Trades were made and then business was a completed by 9 o'clock. After that it was movie time! Boo Baby!

Kid vs. Teenager... Homework time, oh how I hated that time. I fought with you Monday through Thursday on whatever homework assignment you brought home. It started out fine, we would read the directions together on what you were supposed to do and then it began. You wanted to do it your way and I debated back that you can't do it your way, you have to do it according to the directions that are on the top of your paper. We would literally spend 2 hours every afternoon going back and forth on your homework. I would eventually leave the table so I could start dinner and you would sit there in all your stubborn glory. The year you were in first grade was a very frustrating one. I was ready to pull my hair out, but on the flip side I give you some strange props...you were a kid that stuck to your guns and didn't back down. In the end, I learned how to get you to do your homework and save my sanity... no homework, no TV. Bam...homework, reading and chores done in about an hour. Beautiful!

Teenager vs. Teacher... Mom pulled you out of Jr. High because you were getting into too much trouble. Not sure how exactly to help you, she asked if I would be willing to home school you. I thought it over for a minute and said sure. I knew that if there was at least one person you would listen and pay attention to, it would be me. I knew that I could teach you what you needed to know. Plus, I figured that I could also kick that punk attitude of yours out the window where it belonged. So the following week Mom pulled you out of Sitting Bull Jr. High and enrolled you into Options Home Schooling. I'll never forget your face when I told you that school started at nine o'clock. Sharp! That meant that you were dressed, ate breakfast and ready at the kitchen table with your work, pencil and notebooks. You thought I was going to just let you do the work when you felt like it and in your pj's no less...oh silly boy, guess again. See the one thing you forgot in the midst of your happy dance was that I'm a nerdy bookworm who loves education. Your big sister always went above and beyond with school projects and reports. I was the A+ student. Math, English and Art were the first classes before lunch and then history, Spanish and ending the school day with Physical Education. I'll say it; I loved being your teacher, the power felt good. And you have to admit, you learned a lot with me. You learned studying skills, became organized with your work and you learned what it felt like to have pride in doing a good job. Effort pays off. 6th and 7th grade finished. Time for you to enter the social world of higher education... High School. Even though I enjoyed teaching you, you were still a stressful butthead and I was ready for you to go back to public school. I love you man, but sometimes I just want to slap you upside the head (and I have done the Gibbs slap a time or two... or three)

I'm going to pause here and just say that the most interesting and weird moments in my life was watching my little brother transform from a baby... to a toddler who was now walking and talking like a mini human being... to a kid who had his own thoughts and opinions... to a teenager in high school who thought he was a bag of chips and then some. Boys, y'all are some strange humans... cute, but strange. I have loved every psychotic moment. ;)

Scaredy Cat... Yeah, I'm going to start this memory off by apologizing to you. I am so sorry for all those times that I purposely scared the crap out of you. You my dear boy were a victim caught in the middle of a war going on between me, Dad and Alyssa. See it all started with me, as a kid Dad used to sneak up behind me and scare the shit out of me. However, what he didn't prepare himself for was the grasshopper not only rising to the master's level, but surpassing it. The grasshopper was the new master in town. And you know me, I have to perfect the scare war by taking it one level further. I scared Lu a few times, then taught her the tricks of the trade. I needed a new target and your name was next on the list. That night I scared you in the laundry room was classic. You had just got out of the shower, you walked into your room to get dressed which meant that your next stop was the laundry room to put your dirty clothes in the hamper. I stood in the doorway, quietly and patiently waiting for you. The second you turned to enter the room I creepily said, "Boo" and you screamed, slipped and tossed your clothes in the air like confetti. It was hilarious. You would tell me that you were going to get me back and I might have actually been a little cautious, however the number one rule to scaring someone is to NOT tell them when, where and how you plan to get them. It took you a few more times of almost shitting your pants before you realized that. Although you did get me back years later, so we're even.

Movies and Music... Action movies... Horror movies... You are my go to guy. Anytime I see a commercial for a creepy movie, I think to myself, "I gotta tell Zac about this!" Yes, I know that I draw the line with clowns and porcelain dolls, but everything else is fair game. Bring on the evil spirits... bring on the possessed... bring on the haunted. The only clown I can tolerate is The Joker and that's because he's fascinatingly deranged. Front row, feet up, a fresh batch of salty pretzel bites (one for each because we don't know how to share) and a couple of Coke icees...we know how to do movies right. Surprisingly enough, we also have similar tastes in music. You're big with the worlds of rap and country and I'm big in the worlds of rock and alternative, but somewhere in the middle of it all we have mutual bands and songs that we both rock out to. Some of your music picks have become favorites in my playlists and some of my music has become favorites of yours. You're always coming to me with a new song, band or solo artist that you want me to check out. I introduced you to bands like 3 Doors Down, Nickelback, Daughtry, Fall Out Boy, Eminem and Maroon 5. You introduced me to artists like Luke Bryan, Timeflies and Imagine Dragons. You and I are always testing each other's music knowledge... name that band or name that song.

Time to get on a serious level for a moment... even though you and I have had our moments of wanting to kill each other, you have grown into a loving... kind hearted... sensitive... smart and all around awesome man. I can't believe that you're already 18 years old as I'm writing this. I have watched you grow into this newbie adult who has dreams of what his life is going to be like. You have matured so much over the years and I know that someday you are going to make a great husband to a very lucky woman and an amazing dad. Anytime I need help with something, you're there. Anytime I ask you to do something, you do it. I soak in every conversation we have. I treasure the times we take out of our crazy lives to hang out. And yes, I even love the fact that you are just as big of a fan as I am of Pretty Little Liars. That's our show man. ;)

I know that there are times that you feel as though people are judging you, that there are times where you feel as though you need to do what the "in' crowd is doing so that you'll be accepted in society. The stage that you're in right now is a confusing one. It's a time when you're torn between being what others want you to be and who you want to become. Take a minute... Take a breath and listen. You are who you are and as long as you're happy, healthy and in a good place with yourself then the only approval needed is your own. Follow your dreams no matter how outrageous. Set the path of your life the way you want it to go. Don't allow the outside static factor into who you are. Just be Zac, because I know him, he's a pretty cool guy.

Dear Present & Future Me,

Damn girl! How in the world did we survive the hurricane that's been our life? "Everything happens for a reason" has aided in the frustration and insanity that's clouded the path. Music has been the morphine drip numbing the violent vibrations pounding through our mind. Writing has been the escape route taken when running forward every time we've murdered our past. Friends have band-aided small cuts and wounds. Family has been our solid shoulder to shed each black tear, created milestones of happiness and the warm embrace that's comforted our heart.

This frozen moment is picturesque, strokes of brilliance beautifully framed for all the world to see.

Guarded we remain and that's ok because the walls represent that trust is a privilege earned not just freely handed out or bought. Our heart is still under lock and key, but that's ok too because its stitched strength is reserved for the one who deserves its goldenness. Its scars remind us that we will no longer blindly jump into just anyone's arms. Despite these necessary glitches, we're doing just fine (no I don't mean freaked out, insecure, neurotic and emotional).

30 years young, and I must say that you've never looked so beautiful. You've become a force that wakes up every morning, ready to take on the day and every curve ball that may be thrown your way. As for the future, I can't predict what storms may come, I can't reveal if love will kiss your forehead, I can't have loose lips if your story will ever be shared with the world (depending on someone's assistance is a sticky wicket because you're now counting on someone to have the courage to take a chance on a nobody). But, I can spill the secret that the past's ashes will forever reside six feet under, never to darken your starry night.

The only advice that I shall pay you off with is never ever hinder who you are, under any circumstances should you fold. Life only gives you a single game. So, shuffle the deck... Grasp the hand you've been dealt... Shut your eyes... Take a breath... And play those Aces...

Dear Future Hubby,

So this is your future wifey writing you a letter, thought maybe you'd like to know a bit about what you're jumping into. Obviously we haven't met yet, but that doesn't mean you can't get to know me. Ok, so let's dive right into this craziness! ;)

So, I'm going to jump right into my idiosyncrasies, or flaws I guess. Uh, well there's the first weird fact about myself, as a writer I like to use words that aren't normally spoken on a daily basis and I also like to twist words. That's one of the beauties about writing, playing with words and seeing how many different ways you can manipulate them. I have a thing for words, mainly due to the fact that I sometimes have difficulties verbally expressing certain emotions. You will more than likely be much better at that than I. It's not that I don't know how to express those emotions (sadness, anger) I just happen to have a glitch that prevents a smooth transition from thought to verbalization. Imagine someone who is learning to speak English, yeah it's kinda like that. Which leads me to another fun fact, I am pretty closed off. Not to everyone, just towards those who aren't part of my squad. It takes a bit for me to trust outsiders. I've always gone by my golden rule that trust is earned not just handed out like candy on Halloween. Once we get to know one another I will start to open up, I promise. I suppose that I am one of those humans that speak louder in my silence or through my eyes.

I am very independent, which has always been a bittersweet aspect of mine. While I'm not needy, I possess a slim yet empowered stubborn streak. Asking for help is pretty much labeled as plan "ZZ" (I imagine that this would be the letter that comes after Z). I don't get stressed very often, however, when I do you'll know. Headphones with either rock or rap blasting and a hoodie blocking out the world means stay away. One or the other is safe, both together equal "Enter at your own Risk". ;) There is really only one lie that I keep in my back pocket and pull out when needed, "I'm fine". If you ask "Are you ok?" and I respond with "I'm fine", I'm lying my ass off. Any other answer is 100% honest.

I have a tendency to get inside my own head when I'm stressed, it's not a feature I like about myself, but there it is. Hmmm, I think that's about it for my flaws, well the ones I can think of at the moment anyways. Oh crap, sleep and I are not on the best of terms. I am an insomniac, but you'd never know it had I not told you. I'm like a ninja with stealth-like quietness. I sneak softly and tread lightly so you'll still be able to get your beauty sleep.

Now for a dose of awesomeness. I love to cook; whether I'm following a recipe, cooking dishes I grew up on or just Iron Chefing it, delicious food is made. Oh, be prepared, music and me dancing in the kitchen while I cook goes down almost every time. I'm a bookworm, my nirvana is perusing a bookstore while sipping on a latte.

You will have to drag me out, seriously, no joke. ;)
Movies? Absolutely! Comedy, action, romantic, horror...
I love them all. Video games, board games, dancing, art
(drawing, painting, etc.) I like to keep busy. While I
enjoy the outside world of traveling, concerts, museums,
days/nights spent at the beach, spending time with
family and friends, I also enjoy those times where I stay
in and unplug. I guess you could categorize me as both
an extrovert and introvert. I'm also down for new
experiences and adventures that I've never done. Making
memories and snapping photos. Smile! :)

Basic info? Well, I'm 5'6"ish... Brunette with blonde
highlights... hazel eyes... part German and Norwegian
with a few mystery dashes...I'm fun sized. ;) I am an
aspiring writer that manages a blog called Genuinely
Derra, I am a contributing writer for My Trending
Stories and I have a book in the works. Currently I am
working on another manuscript and other pieces as well.

On a personal note, I was born with a rare disorder
called Epidermolysis Bullosa, EB. As much as I wish I
didn't have to mention it, I must due to the fact that there
is a physical aspect to my disorder. My hands look like
fists. I want to state now that I am not looking for you to
take care of me, I have my shit handled. EB is a small
part of my life, it always will be, I can't make it vanish
which I love/ hate. It is in no way a part of who I am
though. Derra is not EB and EB is not Derra. It took me
a while, but I have made EB my bitch. It knows its place.
It doesn't stop me from doing what I want to do or living
my life. In a way, I'm thankful for its presence, this
curse has grounded me, made my levels of empathy
deeper; traits of judgment are not instilled in my brain

and it causes me to constantly push myself to achieve my dreams (sometimes even past the brink, don't worry though, I always find my way back).

Life as a misfit has its pros and cons, much like anything in life. Pro: life is definitely not in any way boring or dull. I've been told that I'm a pretty interesting person (I don't see it, but I won't disagree). Con: I know that physical appearance is the first section of the test that I need to pass before moving forward. Only then do my personality, intelligence or any other traits begin to matter. Can I just say, *That Sucks*! Ok I'm good, just needed to get that out.

I may not be the drop dead gorgeous, beautifully breathtaking or the most sexy chica in the room, but I am frickin' adorable! ;) Think of me as an intelligent witty humorous sarcastic creative evil genius smartass... yes, that's all one awesome title. I'm like a cool graffiti piece of artwork, darkly shaded on the outside, but vibrantly colorful on the inside.

I will love you deeper than you'll ever know... I'll support you with every dream and goal you have for yourself... I'll always have your back... I'll take care of you when you're sick... I'll always find a way to make that frown of yours crack into a grin... I'll sit and listen to every thought you have to say... I'll sit in the silence you want and supply my wisdom if needed... I'll be your safe place, your home... I'll never lie, cheat or make you feel unimportant or unwanted (I know all too well how that feels) ... I'll be your Superwoman <3

Until our paths cross... <3

Xoxo, Boo

P.S. there's a few things I left out of this letter, figured
I'd keep some info classified until we, you know,
actually meet. ;)

Dear Fellow Butterflies,

How's it going my lovelies? I know that a good percentage of you out there in this great big world think that you've been dealt a rotten hand. Hardships and labels stacked in your deck from day one. And yes, I will be the first to admit that it sucks! We can't trade those cards for others and some days I just want to scream until my face is shaded blue. The trick is to learn how to play the cards you have without folding. Epidermolysis Bullosa is definitely one of the most challenging games we play.

I have learned a few key secrets to surviving this whole "being different" life. And here I am, giving you the inside scoop.

Secret #1... The main road block that stops us from living a full life is ourselves. We are born into a bubble wrapped world. Everyone working overtime to protect us from anything that may cause the slightest bump or scrape. Now I am fully aware of the fact that there are several types and sub-types of EB. Some have a simple form while others have a very severe case. I also know that there are certain limitations given in this type of life.

A dangerous side -affect develops when we swallow "delicate" and "fragile" pills day after day. Allowing our limitations to take over creates a fear in our minds that can sometimes prohibit us from stepping outside our front doors and entering into the great unknown. The world can be a scary place, trust me I know. But at the same time, it's a beautiful scene. There is nothing more therapeutic than taking a walk in a park, clearing one's head while swinging on a swing. Smelling the sweet perfume that the flowers spritz into the warm sunny breeze. Or, how about a day at the beach. Hanging with family and friends. Exchanging good conversation, delicious food and awesome music. The warm sand... Cool ocean breeze and the sound of crashing waves. A day that turns into a gorgeous neon sunset, a crackling bonfire and tasty ooey gooey s'mores. Or, my favorite, a gloom and doom day of a clouded sky, a chilly atmosphere and rain drops dancing around you. Ever danced in the rain or jumped in a giant puddle? How about bundling up and going outside to build a snowman on a cold winter's day? Catching snowflakes on your tongue, making a snow angel or having a snowball fight? You can't experience any of this in your house. And it's no fun being the kid on the inside looking out of the window watching everyone else. I'm not assuming that every kid with EB is afraid to step out their front door and major props to the adventurous butterflies out there, but I know some of you are nerve racked at the thought of leaving your bubble. I also know that some parents out there are equally scared to set their kids free. You know what I do when I'm scared to try new things? ... I close my eyes, take a deep breath and ask myself if I'm ready to do this. The answer is usually "Nope... so let's do it anyways". When I was growing up, there were countless times when my Ma' had to close her eyes, take a breath and let go. It's not easy, but it is awesome! A "should have, could have, would have," life isn't a life at all. What doesn't kill us only makes us stronger ;)

Secret #2... Don't Care so much. You can't avoid being stared at when you're out and about enjoying life. It's inevitable. Don't allow public ignorance to turn you into an introvert. Me personally, I don't even notice it 90% of the time. If I do, it doesn't even really phase me. I just look at them and smile. That's all you have to do. Most of the time they will stop, but on the occasion that they won't let up then just simply go up to them and say, "Take a pic, it'll last longer" ;) If you're lucky, sometimes people will approach you with kindness. People that stare are just curious as to what's going on with us and may feel intimidated with coming up and just asking. Not every stare is an arrogant one. Never judge, if you judge them for staring then you're no better than them judging you for your EB. Food for thought there.

Secret #3... It's ok to say "No". Ok so I know I'm about to do a whole "the shits about to hit the fan" scenario here and it will probably drop a few jaws, but I cannot allow myself to keep this undercover because of possible disagreements. As kids our parents and even our doctors, make the decisions about our health care. However, at some point we have to become part of that decision making process. We have a voice, let's use it. A quick warning: sometimes you may have to make your voice boom to get the attention directed towards you.

We have well working brains, let's use them. Only we know what's best for us, only we know how much our bodies can take. If you allow everyone to constantly make the decisions for you then you'll never learn how to make a solid smart decision, which will lead you to lose a huge part of your independence. Needing assistance is inevitable with any disability, but we need to become as independent as we can. It's an important part of life, a huge part of one's happiness. When you know that you're doing what's best for you and not what everyone else wants you to do or what you think is expected of you, then you're going to feel amazing. Of course there are going to be those who won't agree with whatever decision you've made, but what they need to realize is that this is your life, not theirs. Doctors aren't always right. What may work for one person, may not work for another.

Props and high fives all around to those who are getting out there and playing on the ultimate playground. Props and fist bumps to those who are nervous to step out of the door. The fact that you've opened the door and have the taste to get out there, you're halfway there. Just close your eyes... take a deep breath... And take one more step. Courage and strength live inside you...release them baby!

No dream is too outrageous... No wish too extravagant... You are beautiful just the way you are, never let anyone tell you otherwise.

Dear Butterfly Parents,

This is going to be short and sweet because I'm not a parent and I have no clue on how you must feel or what you're going through. I can merely ask that if your kids want to try new experiences that you let them. No matter how terrified you may be, don't shoot their dreams down. It may take some creativity and a few adjustments. But more times than not, a way can be found in helping your kids achieve their goals and dreams. If they see that you're supportive, they'll become more courageous in wanting to be adventurous. If you're less scared and less open, then they'll imitate those same actions. The limitations you set will affect how many limitations they set for themselves. Never start a conversation with "No" ... instead start with "let's see how we can make it happen".

P.S. The darkest nights produce the brightest stars...

Dear Uncle Ricky,

First off I just want to say that you give the best hugs! My earliest memory that I have of you is when I was about to go in for my first hand surgery and you were at the hospital with my parents. You had given me a stuffed purple bunny named Sweet Pea. You told me that she was going to watch over me while I was in surgery. Since I couldn't take her in the O.R. with me you held on to her.

I also remember the time my Ma and Dad dropped me off at your house because they were going to my Popee's Company Christmas party (liquor = no kids... lol). We watched the Charlie Brown Christmas Special, colored and you had made Cream soda floats. Who knew that vanilla ice cream and cream soda were so good together? I also got to play with Nick and hold him. It's weird that we're all grown adults now. I loved when we got to hang out.

I know that after my family and I moved to the high desert we didn't get to see each other a whole lot. A lot of years flew by and families grew. Once in a while we were able to make it to Nick's Birthday parties and visa-versa. Schedules were constantly chaotic. Years later

Facebook made it much easier to keep in contact. I love how you always know what I'm up to before I tell you.

During one conversation on the phone we had decided to plan times to get together. Sometimes life needs to be planned and placed on the calendar. This seems to work better for us than just trying to wing-it. I always look forward to our yearly beach trip during the summer. I've also noticed that there's always good eats when we all get together. Whether we're grilling up some of your delicious chicken, hot dogs (your favorite) or cheesy burgers. It's always a delicious time. Even if we all decide to eat out, a great restaurant is picked.

You had said something at one of yours and Aunt Debs Fourth of July parties that stuck with me… you would rather have a small group of friends that you actually have relationships with than a hundred acquaintances that you hardly know. So true. Too many people these days want that popularity status of "knowing" all these people. Words of wisdom from the Godfather ;)

It's always a good time when I get to spend time with you, Aunt Deb and Nick. Or as I call you guys…My favorite humans... lol. Laughs, intelligent conversations and good times always go down when you're all around.

I am honored to have you all in my life. It definitely wouldn't be the same without y'all.

Dear Popee,

I miss you Popee. I know it's been nearly eight years since you've passed, however there are moments from time to time that feel freshly broken. I think it's because I never actually got to say goodbye to you... or worse, that I never got the chance to tell you that I loved you one last time. That damn fear I have with hospitals, I allowed it to get in my way. That Saturday afternoon that my Mom, Alyssa and I went to St. Mary's to check up on you shouldn't have gone down the way it did. I should have been in your room, at your side, being there for you. All those times that you were unconditionally present, I should have been there. It was the moment to repay you for all that you've done. Instead, I play a game of chicken. Barely able to step one foot past the doorway into your hospital room. A small glance of you lying in that bed, hooked to machines, looking more fragile than I. My foot stepped back and I start to break down in the hallway. I told Mom that I had to go home, that I couldn't be there. I left, stupidly thinking that I would have time to come back. That I would have time to get over myself so that I could be there for you. Selfishness is all I could portray that afternoon. Sunday wasted away and Monday arrived. Mom and I went back to the hospital to see you and this time I was determined place my fear on the back burner and concentrate on what was important. Company occupied your bed side from other

83

family members, so Mom and I gave them some time and decided to come back after running a few errands. A few hours passed. Sitting in the car going thru the Taco Bell drive through I received the call. It was Auntie Pam. The second I saw her name appear on my cell phone screen I knew. Back to the hospital we went. Mom went in to talk to the Doctors and I stayed in the car with Zach. I cried, I had foolishly expected that time would be on my side so that I could do what I should have done from the beginning. I wasn't at your bed side, even though you weren't always coherent, I think you would have known if I was there. I didn't have the chance to say one final goodbye... or I love you. The next few weeks were a whirlwind. The last two weeks of October faded into November and then into December. Holidays feeling emptier, my sadness morphing into anger. Goodbye isn't a word one likes to say when there's not an inevitable return.

December 6th bit me like a rattler. Santa Monica Beach is where family gathered. A prayer was read amongst tearful hearts... Flower petals freed into the ocean, swaying as they traveled further into the distance... A sand castle was built and half of your ashes were spread into the moat (along with Nana's ashes). Waves crashed over the castle and swallowed it into the big blue. The chilly beach air was so therapeutic... calming... Goodbye Popee... I Love You.

Old photographs led to mini movies playing in my head which led to a smile finally becoming present. Days at the beach collecting seashells. Trips to the "hardware store" to get a buttery pecan treat.

Amazement and wonder watching the prismatic Electrical Parade at Disneyland. Afternoons planting baby flowers.

Dreams of you and I having coffee at the local coffee house (we do love a good cup of coffee), conversing on how life was going. Dream after dream… coffee after coffee… The last time we met in the alternate world you had told me to forgive myself. You told me that I was wasting precious time being angry over events that I had no control over. You knew how much I was grateful for everything… you knew how much I wanted to be there at the hospital… and you knew that I loved you. We stood up from our chairs, hugged and went our separate ways. I woke up with a lighter feeling invading my mind. My mission was to ace your final wish to me… move forward.

After our final coffee meeting I only saw you in my dreams if I needed a bit of direction for the road I was currently driving down. You helped me let go of the issues I had with Nana and you warned me with a glimpse of what life would be like remaining in a toxic relationship. Even though you weren't living on planet earth anymore, you still protected me.

I am happy to report that I am doing splendidly. I got lost and turned around a few times, but was always able to find my way back. Forward is where I'm looking… the past is no longer a place I hit rock bottom in. It's a tool that I use so I won't repeat history. I think of you from time to time, certain specks of life pop your image into my head. Butter pecan ice cream… a cold beer… The Philadelphia Eagles… Bourbon sausages at the holidays… and every day that I wear my lucky charm necklace (your dog tag from your Navy days), my frown is permanently turned upside down. Thank You Popee.

Dear Aunt Betty,

I want to start off by saying that I am truly honored to be your Hunny Bunch #4. You have always held a special place in my heart Aunt Betty. As I grew older I learned that your heart is made of pure kindness, generosity and unconditional love. Out of all the vacations that my family and I had taken, traveling to Pennsylvania was hands down my favorite place to visit. Yep, I couldn't wait to visit you and Uncle Herm. Living in the city is fast paced and noisy, but I love it because it distracts me from the chaos in my mind. The relaxed pace of Lebanon, Pa. is calming. A therapeutic sense washed over me the second I'd step in your house. A small part of me feels as though I will never truly belong in this world, but you always had a way of shutting that switch off. Every time that I visited you always planned a trip to the Jubilee shop for a little shopping... Hershey Park's Chocolate World, the smell of chocolate swims through the air, so tasty and of course the pretzel shop for freshly baked giant soft pretzels. I loved watching the guys in the back twist the dough into the pretzel shape, place them into the oven and pull the ones that were done out. That shop smelled so good. There's nothing like dough baking, whether it's bread, pretzels, doughnuts... it's all delicious. During the summer, we would make a trip up to Donna and Nate's farm. And no trip back east was complete without going to Amish Country. The shops of homemade goods and the food... oh the food (my favorite part).

My fondest memory with you is the time that my Mom and I came to visit a year after Popee passed away. Saturday morning I woke up to the smell of your delicious blueberry pancakes, my absolute favorite. After breakfast you, Mom and I went down to the Jubilee shop to do a little shopping, then off to the market to pick up a couple of things for lunch and lastly back to the house. A gloomy raining sky blanketed over the town. That night I made dinner... Vodka pasta with garlic bread and salad. I used Uncle Herms Cherry wine in the sauce. He told me that you have to dig to the bottom of the pot to get the good stuff. Dinner was done and the dishes were cleaned. 7 o'clock came, which of course meant dessert time on the back porch. I believe it was a slice of your scrumptious fruit cake (not the cinder block kind. This fruit cake is the real deal!) Later that night my Mom had gone to bed and Uncle Herm was watching the playoff game on TV. You and I were sitting at the table, talking recipes as you showed me all the old family recipes you had saved over the years. Snacking on peanut butter Ritz crackers and a glass of milk, we chatted up into the late hours of the night. The conversation turned into how I was doing. How I was handling Popee's passing. I had told you that it was hard letting go, but that I was starting to become ok with everything. I also told you that I had a strange feeling about a week before Popee passed. A strange twisted tingling feeling in the pit of my stomach. I had also had the same feeling a week before Nana died. I exposed to you the dreams I was currently having. Feeling like a freak confessing all of this, you looked at me with that sweet face of yours and shared your priceless wisdom. "Pay attention to your feelings and dreams. They may be premonitions. Don't doubt them and don't be afraid of them." Those words were like a kind slap to my brain... my thought bubbles filled with intrigue. I had never doubted any advice you gave me when I was little and I wasn't going to now. I guess when you feel like an outcast, any other problems that come your way you just want to sweep them under the rug. Out of sight, out of mind.

As we hugged and turned in for the night, I laid in bed thinking of what you had said, which led me down a night of nostalgia. Past dreams I had had since I was a kid... were they just my over active imagination taking over or where they more? The next day we all woke up and got ready for church. The skies were crystal blue and the sun was warming the October chill. After church we went back to the house for lunch with everybody. It seemed like the whole gang was there. Nikki, Keith, Josh, Tammy, George, Linda, Tom, myself, Mom, you and Uncle Herm. Lunch ended and everyone was headed to the cemetery were great Grandma and Grandpa Donmoyer lay to rest. Some of Popee's ashes were being placed with them. I had decided to stay back. I just couldn't do the whole "Goodbye" thing again. I felt bad because I thought I should have gone for you, but you told me that you understood. I had said my goodbyes to my Popee, it was now your turn to say goodbye to your brother. By the end of the weekend, all tears were able to turn golden. Monday morning came and "I love You" was said as my Mom and I departed back to Cali. I think that trip helped me to actually allow myself to stitch together the brokenness. It's crazy, but a four day trip to visit you melted away any stress that was invading the days. I would always get back home and feel like my worries were minor. You made me feel like an insider, you taught me what family value is and most importantly that life is all about the simple things. I am forever grateful.

Dear Nightmares,

Eleven years old… the first time I had a nightmare. The first night of many to follow where sleep and I would no longer be friends. They say that nightmares and dreams are your sub-conscience working out issues you may be having. Even though you're sleeping, your brain is awake and running. Working out any stresses, issues or concerns you may have. Dreams are the gateway to any excitements and wonders going on in your day world. Nightmares are your stresses, old demons and fears haunting your night world. Now I'm certainly no expert on the topic of dreams vs. nightmares, but I will tell you that after 19 years of living the nocturnal life of insomnia, my nightmares and I have become frenemies.

As a kid, nightmares are terrifying. You're not sure what they mean or why you're having them. All you know is that now you're afraid to go to sleep because if you do you'll just have another bad dream. And that's exactly what I went through. I never told my parents that I was having these horrible dreams; I had enough problems that people seemed to have the need to fix. I didn't want to add my brain to the list. So, I kept my mouth shut. These insane plots would play in my head like a horror movie. Strange places that I had never seen… strange creatures that lived there. Knowing that these dreams had their own itinerary on when they'd pop into my head made it difficult to sleep. I figured that if I stayed awake then I couldn't dream. It's a solid plan, however a wrench is thrown into it when the sandman comes and makes your eyelids extremely heavy. Eventually they shut and you spin off to nightmare land. It was hard getting up for school in the mornings. The odd thing is that after a few months of having these creepy nightmares, I started to become used to them. They kind of became a part of my life. The more I visited these strange places the more I felt comfortable. The creatures that resided there were different, like me. Think of The Island of Misfit Toys plus Nightmare Before Christmas with a pinch of Texas Chainsaw Massacre. I know, sounds absolutely bizarre and freaky. Guess what, it was.

Now I know that sometimes kids grow out of having nightmares. I did not. Nope, as I got older my nightmares just got creepier and more complex. My Elementary and Jr. High years were filled with the strange worlds that I strangely became accustomed to. In High School my nightmares faded, and it's not because I grew out of them. It's because High School was a nightmare all on its own. I needed my nights back... I needed sleep to become my friend so that I could survive the days of hell. Graduation came and so did a sigh of relief. That relief didn't last long. My nightmares returned, and somehow they had evolved.

The places were familiar, the people were familiar, the things I did were not. I was murdering people I knew... a masked man in my nightmare world was controlling me and had turned me into a killer. Sleep and I were definitely no longer friends. Every dream interrupted by fear of what I might do next. Each one ending with eyes wide open, heart about to pound out of my chest and lungs gasping for oxygen. Do you know what it's like to wake, shaking in a cold sweat? If you don't, be thankful because that's a feeling that I don't wish upon anyone. If you are also someone who gets a good night's sleep, be thankful for that too. Over the years I have learned that sleep is a privilege.

I had one advantage this time around... knowledge! I had done research and learned that killing someone in your dreams doesn't actually mean "killing". If you look up the meaning of "killing" in a dream book, it refers to an ending. The ending of a certain phase in your life, the ending of a relationship with someone. Ending these things so that you can move forward. The only thing that I didn't understand was the attendance of the masked man. I would have the same reoccurring nightmare five or six times before a continuation would present itself. The cold sweats were the unwanted prize at the end of each new installment. After the second one, just a jolting awake-ness occurred. Even though I wanted nothing to do with my nightmares, these too became a part of my night world resulting in the return of my nocturnal life of insomnia.

Years later, the masked man was unveiled... any guesses as to who he was? I'm just going to give you the answer because in order to be able to even be close to the correct answer, you would have to know a certain part of my history that I don't believe I have shared before this point. The masked man was my biological father. Boom! Mind blown and jaw dropping right. Yep, my Dad entered my Mom's and mine life when I was about a year and a half. Keith Sabo is my Dad and always will be, just not on a biological level. His name is Jonathan. I know a little info about him and what went down, there's a letter dedicated to that impact as well.

The masked man dreams seemed to fade as I came to conclusion that I needed to let all of my unanswered questions stay unanswered. I'm someone who needs to know why, what, where, when and how. It's hard for me to let go of the unknown, but it's needed every once in a while.

More dreams were encountered. Mostly the same terrifying scenarios. Good dreams were sprinkled in from time to time. With every bad or good dream, I study each and every one to figure out what the hidden meaning is. Is my over active imagination getting the best of me or is this a puzzle piece to the bigger picture of something to come?

My past demons... My unanswered questions… they equal my nightmares. At this point, I think a piece of me would be missing if they stopped interrupting my nights. Makes perfect sense… doesn't it?

Dear Bullies,

Well here we are. This letter goes out to all of you who would take your own problems out on me. To those who painted a target one my forehead and to those who fired all of your sharp words. To those who tore me down, word by word. You picked on me for being the freak walking around school campus. You called me the science experiment from biology class. You told me that I was damaged goods. You picked, teased, made fun of and casted me to a social life on the outs. Frustration and tears were wasted on your hurtfulness. High School was the worst. Those four years were turned into hell because of you. Clubs were not joined... Dances and Prom were not attended... My mission was to get through 6 classes a day and make it to graduation. At the end of all the unnecessary bullshit you rained on me I have just one thing to say to all of you... Thank You.

You weren't expecting that were you? Well, there it is. Every rumor spread... Every mean-spirited name called... Every time you tore me down... it just added to the strength that I have today. The stares I receive when I'm out living my life don't even phase me. Darkened words ping off of the armor that you helped me build. Throw your sticks and stones... throw your sharp words... ain't not a thing, but a chicken wing baby.

Call me a name; I'll just look at you with a look of boredom. If you're going to take the time to call me something hurtful, at least be creative. Just don't get butt hurt when I laugh at it.

I know who I am… what you outsiders think doesn't matter. It's all white noise that disappears into the breeze.

So, that's all I have to say. Don't get me wrong. I could sit here and type every dirty detail of what went down and play of game of revenge, but I'm not that type of person and to be honest, you don't deserve more than this page dedicated to you. I bid you no ill will and I hope that any bitterness that you once held in your heart is gone.

Dear John Doe,

This is an extremely belated *Congratulations*, but better late than never. I hear your girlfriend just gave birth to a baby girl. Wow! You're a father now. I bet you're very excited. The relationship between a father and daughter is precious. You are her first love... her superhero... you'll be the one who protects her from the monsters under her bed and teach her how boys should treat her as she enters the dating world, cheering her on as she walks across that stage to accept her diploma and see her off to college. You'll be there to wipe her tears away during her first heartbreak and walk her down the aisle on her big day. Creating endless memories with Daddy's little girl, becoming her best friend when she's grown.

I'd like to take a moment to say that I know you must be nervous beyond words, especially since your daughter was born with a very rare disorder. Through the grape vine I have been passed along the details that it's Epidermolysis Bullosa. Doctors say that there's practically no information on that disorder, in fact only one case has been seen previous to your baby's. Guaranteed concerns that she will suffer from mental disabilities along with the physical. Brain mentality will likely stop progression at the level of a toddler's. Life expectancy is 14 years or less. News that no parent should have to hear after "Congratulations, it's a girl!"

Two weeks spent in the ICU... now she's home with you both, I'm ecstatic to hear that. A couple months have passed, how are things? How's that beautiful baby girl of yours? You're not sure, why not? Oh... you've left your girlfriend and baby. Oh.... why? Were you too overwhelmed with the abundant amount of information that the doctors threw at you? Did you just not want to be a part of the responsibilities of being a father. Or, perhaps, you didn't want to have to deal with a damaged kid. Whatever the reasoning, it's a shame you're gone.

Well, I can confirm that your baby girl is grown, healthy and if I may add, an intelligent witty sarcastic adorable smartass. ;) This awesome freak has had quite the journey, a few times she's fallen while constantly picking herself up. There was a period of time when giving up was a constant thought swimming through her busy mind, but an outside force has kept her going. As for the mental disability, well that was never an issue. During Kindergarten she tested at the 3rd grade level for Math and English. While most kids were learning to print their names, she could handwrite hers. She graduated high school in 3 years with a 4.0 GPA. Turns out she is one smart little cookie. As for the physical disability part, well, her hands look like two fists, but she doesn't allow anything to prevent her from doing whatever she wants. This chick is one determined human being, always leaving "asking for help" as a last resort. She'll push herself and failure is not an option in her world. She found her voice in becoming a writer. From blogging to writing a book about all of her life encounters, forming a career pathway to help and inspire.

I'd like to take one more moment to say that your absence caused several periods of mental and identity struggles. A life lived with only knowing 50% of her origin. Caught in a spiral of unanswered questions. 1/2 German, 1/8 Norwegian & 3/8 of *??????* The capability to only fill out her Mother's side on the medical history form. Only able to build half of a family tree in school. Secretly feeling like the odd man out in family photos. You have no idea what that poor girl went through knowing that half of her own blood didn't love her enough to stick around and give her a chance to prove all those so called statistics wrong. 31 years of breaking rules and defying every odd. Yeah, you heard right, she is 31 years old. Guess death at 14 wasn't approved by her.

Applause for you though. Why? you may ask. Well, a couple years after you left, your ex-girlfriend met an amazing man who fell in love with her and that invincible baby girl. A flower girl at the age of 3 ½ is what that little girl had the honoring of being at her parents' wedding. 6 years old, sitting on her Dad's lap in a courtroom, listening as the judge approved the adoption. A family now built, forever creating memories together. Years down the road that family of three grew to a family of five.

Even though your baby never knew you, you always were and always be a permanent blank space in her mind. Turns out that after all is said and done, now at the end of the yellow brick road, you gave her the best gift she's ever received in her life... you left.

I'm not sure where you reside these days or the kind of person you've become, but that's ok. You made your choice all of those years ago to abandon ship and I've made my decision to let go and forgive you.

Sincerely,

Baby Girl

Dear Nana,

I wasn't originally going to include a letter to you in this book. Mainly for two reasons. One, I don't have the greatest of memories with you. The words manipulating and evil come to mind (sounds bad but that's the truth. No sense in sugar coating it). Two, you're no longer with us and I felt like this may turn into a grudge letter. Exuding my grievances and just plain old being pissed at all of the unanswered questions you ducked out on. So instead, I'm going to look towards the brighter side and share the life lessons that you taught me.

First lesson... Don't put Baby in a corner. I remember the times when I was a kid and I'd visit you and Popee during my school vacations. My Dad would drop me off at your house and I'd spend the day with you. You would take me shopping, take me to the movies and we would always meet up with Popee for lunch. Now one would think to themselves that this sounds like a great "Granddaughter and Grandmother" day. Except for one small glitch. See, I quickly learned that your niceness came with a price tag attached. Clothes and movies were purchased in exchange for information about my parents that I didn't have. After the fun stuff was over it was interrogation time... Like clockwork every time. I was 10... what 10-year-old knows anything about their parent's financial business.

NONE! I used to go home and tell my Mom that you were asking me certain questions about her and Dad. I asked her what I should say the next time it happens because my "I don't know" answer was losing as evidence. The next visit came with another interrogation and I fired the ammo that Mom supplied me with. Each question asked was given the answer, "I'm not sure. Ask my Mom." Not an answer you liked, but I did get you to let up on asking me things that I had no knowledge of.

Lesson learned... You don't portray yourself as a nice person and toss out bribes to get something in return. Dishonesty gets you nowhere.

Second Lesson... Never let your guard down. I'm a smart cookie and you would have known that had you ever paid attention. Instead you implemented your evil little plans to place a wedge between my Mom and I. The one time I let my guard down with you, the one time I think that you're genuinely being a nice person and it results into a slap in the face (not literally). Every visit you would take me to a movie. You would circle the choices I could choose from in the newspaper. Nothing over the PG Rating was allowed and that made sense. I was 13 at the time, so I got the whole "appropriate" movie deal. Well that day came when shockingly you handed me the newspaper and said that I could pick any movie I wanted. No restrictions attached. Amazed and a bit dazed by this confusing generosity, I chose to go see Rush Hour. That movie was rated "R", and I knew that I wasn't allowed to see it, but I was taking advantage of this rare moment. Before we left to go to the theaters and lunch, I went into the restroom to wash up. Stupidly on my part, I figured that you would have called my Mom to double check on the "green light" for seeing Rush Hour. I didn't ask if you did and you didn't say. After we had lunch at Sizzler with Popee, he went back to his office and we went to the movies. I loved Rush Hour. Chris Tucker and Jackie Chan were hilarious. That night I told Mom and Dad about my day with you during dinner. When the subject of movies came up, let's just say my Mom's face started to turn a pale shade of red. She wasn't too pleased to hear that you took me to a rated "R" movie without her permission. The end result of letting my guard down and not seeing the manipulative move you were making in your twisted chess game was two weeks of being grounded to my room.

Lesson Learned... Fool me once, shame on you. Fool me twice, shame on me. I guess a leopard really doesn't change its spots.

Teenage years come with a package of wisdom. We become alert to fake backstabbers. As I grew older in age you started to change the game. Instead of trying to get to my Mom through me, I became your sole target. I suppose that you weren't too happy when the little monster you tried to create turned on you and learned the word "No". There's one small fact that you failed to factor into your game strategy, I am a quick learner and I know how to rapidly flip the game into my favor.

Third Lesson... Don't hate the Player, Hate the Game.

After my high school graduation... After the eye surgeries... After all of the rehabilitation I went through I was so stoked to start my college life. I was looking at Michigan University, New York University and Yale. For a whole entire year any time there was a family gathering, what should have been a nice greeting of "Hello" from you was turned into a "Did you apply to any colleges in California?" snare. My reply of "No" was then met with the end of our conversation. I knew that your game plan was to give me the cold shoulder until I went into the direction you wanted me to go into. You pushed every time and I pushed back. My eyes were wide open to everything you were doing. I flew to NY, took a couple of tests and was told that I would hear back from them within 6 to 8 weeks. Two weeks later my acceptance letter came in the mail. My excitement flew across the country. Nothing could stop me now. I was New York University bound. Mom called you and Popee to tell you the good news. A thirty second phone call ended in a letter sent to me three weeks later stating that I was disowned from the family. My college fund was sent to me and instructions that I was to refer to you as Marilyn were singed at the bottom of this cowardly letter.

Lesson Learned... Blood isn't always thicker than water.

Fourth Lesson... Bitterness never dies. New York bound slipped into quick sand. I was now California bound. The news arrived that you and Popee were both sick. To a point where reinforcements were needed. Mom drove to Arizona and took care of you and Popee for three months until her and my Dad moved you guys out to California, near us. And by near us I mean 15 minutes away. During those three months that you had my Mom hostage to your needs, I was at home holding down the fort. My Dad was working his butt off, like he always does and I was taking care of the house needs and Alyssa and Zach. After everything you did to my Mom and to me, her and I worked together to help take care of you. Once you were back in California, I buried all the hate I had towards you and put on the outfit of the dotting Granddaughter. I tattooed a faker than fake smile on my face and pitched in. Family dinners... smiled. Afternoons spent together running errands... smiled.

The night the paramedics came and took you to the hospital was twisted. I comforted my sister since her and I were there when they came. The time that you were in the hospital... I was there, doing whatever needed to be done. Helping my Mom with anything she needed. And did it with a smile. I smiled until the early morning that you passed away. I smiled for Popee to comfort him. I thanked everyone who came up to me at your funeral and gave their condolences. I kept it together when a few of your friends came up to me telling me that all they ever heard you say was how proud of me you were. Funny, I never heard that come out of your mouth once.

Lesson Learned... You don't turn your back on family, even when they do. (this was a lesson my mother taught me... Not you)

Fifth Lesson... Let it go. You passed away leaving several people with unanswered questions as to why you treated them the way you did. Why you were so mean and vengeful. Was it something we did? Or, were you just that bitter? There's only one question left unanswered that I had... What kind of Grandmother treats her Granddaughter the way you did? It took me awhile to let it go, but I did. I knew that I would never get an answer, so it was either allowing the unknown eat at me or bury that son of a bitch. I dug deep and tossed that bad boy six feet under. I knew that I did nothing wrong. I was just the pawn in your game. Used... that's all. I let it all burn along with that jellyfish letter you wrote me.

Final lesson... Find the light in the darkness. I had to look for the good so that I would let go of you. Because of you I love going to the Theater. You took me to see Beauty and The Beast, Peter Pan, The Nutcracker and Where the Wild Things Are (I think that one was an opera). My love for the fine arts is credited to you. I also have a love for fine dining. I know proper dinner etiquette and how to navigate the table setting. And lastly, you were there for some of my surgeries I had when I was a kid.

You taught me how not to treat people. You taught me first- hand what it feels like to be played. To be manipulated and to be tossed aside. I cried when you passed, but not for the reasons I should have. All of this and I still had nothing but respect for you. Simply because you were my Grandmother and you deserved nothing less. I have forgiven you, but I will never forget.

Dear World,

Well, you and me, we've been through the ringer and back. Times of happiness and pauses of heartache. A multitude of lessons were learned and an abundance of wisdom was gained. Kindness... Generosity... Family... Love. Axes that aid in the spinning of life.

A kind word can wipe away a single tear before it falls. A kind thought can lead to a kind gesture that can turn someone's day from darkness to glowing. Even if only for a moment... that moment makes a difference. A kind helping hand quickly multiplies into communities getting together and making neighborhoods beautiful.

An act of generosity is a small pebble tossed, generating a continuous ripple that keeps this beautiful world spinning round and round. A surplus of time given ... a helping hand... A vacant shoulder to lean on... an available ear to bare another's words... a donation of overtime finances to those without... A warm shelter built... a hot meal to fill an empty stomach... a connecting heart to aid in repairing the broken ones. Generosity takes shape in all forms, random souls healing each other... One human at a time.

Family is strength that endures eternal changes and challenges. The Golden list that we turn to when in need of knowledge in an uncertain situation... the lighthouse guiding us through our storms, lighting the way to shore... the ones we enjoy good times with, creating frozen memories that will exist for generations... bailing one another out of stickiness... laughing until pain sets in... tears exposed... matches gone down in the "slammed door" ring. Being a part of your family is the greatest and most difficult journey taken in life. No matter how dysfunctional or insane, family is always there. Yes, times of brokenness may occur, but know that it can always be repaired. Family extends past the blood line... Family are the people whom you mutually love, respect and trust. The ones that you can be your true self with.

Love... a Rubik's Cube of pure terrifying, addicting, intoxicating befuddlement. Seriously! It's like a Romance, Mystery, Comedy and Action thriller all-in-one film. But, you know what... It's the #1 movie worldwide. Continually earning an infinite and priceless rating. Or if you prefer a different scenario, love is like the ultimate road trip.

When you are lucky enough to find the love of your life, hold on to them with everything you have. Love them for all of who they are and give them everything you are. The road of love is a two-way highway my lovelies, from beautifully breath-taking scenery to potholes in the road, but every mile of the trip is infinitely worth it. So love completely, flaws and all. Never pick apart one's heart and think that you can change out what you don't fancy. Love, I give it two thumbs up.

During my past and present years of getting to know this world, I have witnessed times were all four of these trades have assembled to create an untouchable force. September 11, 2001... intruders broke into our home and kidnapped our family. The world stood still, frozen in a moment of shock and awe. Simultaneously collapsing concrete and hearts. Lives ruthlessly taken. Minutes... hours... days... months and years of unrequited pain. It's through Kindness, generosity, family and love that we were able to stand up, brush ourselves off and gather the strength to repair, rebuild and take back our home. Strength in numbers leading to a day of remembrance more than just once a year. Honoring the lost souls and heroes of that darkened day.

You're amazing world... never change <3

Dear Ma',

I end my trip down memory lane with you. I know you'll agree when I say that you and I have had quite the road trip together. Miles of highways blurred by in a blink. Sights of laughter, frustrations, advice, smiles and tears all taken in with every breath-taking sunset. New beginnings and fresh starts brewed with every sunrise. This whole uncertain idea started in a single moment of losing the grip on my beating life. A Denny's parking lot breakdown of tears. Your comforting embrace temporarily numbing my brain from implosion. No one likes swallowing the taste of bad news before they've had their cup of coffee along-side a stack of fluffy pancakes. But you were there, like you always are, to make life a little sweeter. After breakfast we came home and we talked in your room. We discussed the situation that lay on the table and what next possible moves I could play out. After a problem-solving chat I fell asleep on your bed, exhausted from the traffic jam going on in my mind. As I slept I dreamt... dreamt of all the best memories during my life. It was like a mini flashback marathon playing on a projector...

The night before my first day of Kindergarten, you were preparing me for any unkind remarks that the other kids may speak. "Ewww! What happened to you?" ...

The comment that threw me off my guard as it slipped from your lips. Upset as to why you had just said that to me. "I'm not saying it to you to hurt your feelings. I'm saying it because that's what some kids may say to you." My moment of confusion led to realizing that some kids are going to make fun of me because I'm different. That's one of the things I love about you Ma', you always tried to prepare me for the curveballs life might have thrown my way.

You always knew how to plan an awesome birthday party. From the cutest birthday dresses you bought me (gotta look good ☺), to a tasty buffet of food and a variety of refreshing beverages. Fun and entertainment with all sorts of games plus prizes and goodie bags for all, no losers here… lol. Every year was a different theme, from a Halloween costume B-day party to a Barbie party. Parks, restaurants or our house, family and friends filled whichever place with fun and good times. You filled every party with love and awesomeness.

Holidays are my favorite time of the year because of you… lights glowing on the house outside like the front of a Hallmark card, a beautifully decorated Christmas tree, smells of cinnamon and nutmeg wafting throughout the house and Christmas carols concerting from the stereo. My absolute favorite part was setting up the platform. Unboxing each house and shop, the tiny people that resided in this holiday town, setting up the train and watching it click clack on the track. The final touches were sprinkling the snow around the village and plugging it in so that all the houses and shops could glow from their tiny windows.

Beach babies forever... now most people hit the beach in the wee hours of the morning to perhaps catch the sun give its morning greeting or catch the waves at their prime. Some arrive at the beach in the late afternoon to party through the night. The Sabo's hit the beach all day long. Planned out trips to get a primo spot and fire pit in the A.M., ice chests filled with food and drinks, chairs and a pop up canopy for optimum shade, a roll of toilet paper (just in case) and of course s'mores supplies. Friends and family texted the details. Hours of swimsuits, sunscreen, cool waves and warm sand shifted into a blazing fire, hoodies and sticky deliciousness. The perfect remedy to cure the cabin fever driving us mad during the winter.

If you and I were given a dollar for every hour spent at a doctor's office or hospital, we would be millionaires (not a dramatization). Check-ups, lab work, consultations or surgeries... we've spent many a day in waiting rooms. You never once complained or made me feel like an inconvenience. You always found a way to distract me from getting inside my own head, especially when waiting to be taken to the O.R. Words were spoken to make the time pass and comforting silence when I was too nervous, in which case I had my headphones in because during my teenage years only loud music blaring my eardrums could drown out my own apprehension. Anytime I felt like a broken toy, you'd put me back together. P.S. the one time you weren't able to be with me at the hospital for one of my surgeries everything possible went wrong, so lesson learned

there... Mom's get it right, nerve racked teenagers don't
;)

I love when we have our girls' days or nights. Time that you and I spend together and share what's been going on in our crazy schedules. Time without anyone needing anything from us. Time to catch the newest chick flick that just came out, eat at our favorite restaurants (panda express, olive garden or the roadhouse, love their ribs) and do a little shopping. It's my time to inform you of certain things going on and ask for your advice. A few hours of other obligations put on hold. I always thought it was so cool that you always seemed to know when I needed some "Mom" time growing up. A girl loves it when she wakes up on a Saturday morning and her Mom asks her if she wants to hit the mall or movies after breakfast.

Props to you Lady! I knew that you were a busy woman, but I learned first-hand just how psycho a Mom's life is when you went back to school for your Ultra Sound License. A daily routine of waking kids up (which is its own task), getting them ready for school, making breakfast and lunches, dropping kids off at school and coming home. Then part two begins of my own homework, laundry, dishes, tidying up the house and then back to school to pick up the little monsters. Part three of the day includes snacks, arguing over homework, arguing over chores, making dinner and getting all tiny people ready for bed. An hour of whatever is on the Disney channel and then snoozeville. Holy Crap! I felt levels of exhaustion that I never knew existed. Those few months that you were in Arizona

113

taking care of Nana and Popee were crazy too. Running errands was added to the already endless list. Shopping for groceries, house supplies, things that the kids needed for school is a lot different than shopping for shoes and clothes. Making lists of what needed to be done from day to day, school events, football practice and everything else. I don't know how you do what you do, but you do it with pizazz lady. Looking back on all of that insanity, I have to say two things.

1- I'm glad that I was there to help you out with everything. You were always there for me and I felt grateful that I could be there for you.

2- I think that I'll make a pretty badass mom, just sayin'.

Foodies? Oh yes! When it comes to food, whether we're cooking up creations in the kitchen or going out and enjoying the restaurant atmosphere, we love food. There's no hiding or denying it. If we go out and try new dishes, we'd always try to figure out the ingredients so that we could recreate it at home. Cooking up a storm in the kitchen is my favorite, I think I spend way too much time in the kitchen on a daily basis. There's a process to cooking at meal at the Sabo house.

Step one- crank up the tunes. Music is a necessary tool when cooking.

Step two- gather all pots, pans and cooking utensils needed to create a delicious concoction.

Step three- peruse the cupboards and fridge for any and all tasty ingredients.

Step four- turn up the heat and sizzle baby. Dancing and snacking are also allowed while in the kitchen zone.

Tasting your entrée during the cooking process is a must to ensure the proper level of "mouth-watering" is reached. Once it's time to eat the table is then set with plates, silverware, glasses, family and conversation.

Vacation is needed... stat! You planned vacations like nobody's business. Trips to Pennsylvania, New York, Arizona, Las Vegas, Michigan, Seattle, Washington D.C. and my favorite The Mexican Riviera cruise where we traveled to Mazatlán, Cabo and Puerta Vallarta. Sights and experiences of America's vast history, a majestic Grand Canyon, Amish Country simplicity, Manhattan madness and ancient cultures are photographed in my love of travel. Let's take a plane (I've got the window seat) or how about we travel by train and soak in the beautiful scenery. It's always a picture worthy adventure.

A regular Martha Stewart... I admire how you're so crafty. I remember when you used to make my Halloween costumes when I was a kid. I always had the best-looking costumes, so much better than store bought. Batgirl, She-Ra, and Halloween Barbie... I always looked ghoulishly stylish in my Carla Originals. Then there were those weekends when Dad was off umpiring baseball tournaments out of town and you'd paint our bedrooms. Mine was a sunny yellow with a golden yellow splattered on top of it. Lu's was painted bright pink with accents of purple and lime green, Zac's was bright blue with a deeper blue puffed onto it. I loved going to Home Depot to peruse the paint samples and pick colors out for whatever new project you had planned. It was a blast splatter painting the bathroom cupboard doors and the doors to the game room. The game room turned out looking sick painted orange and black and the bathroom transformed into an underwater world of SpongeBob. Our house was the place to hang. I also remember that one summer when you and Zac built that giant dog house for Crash and Shadow. It was huge! Us kids even painted that, it was a summer project you planned. Each of us got a side to paint whatever we wanted, you always let our imaginations run wild. I had the front of the doghouse and I painted to look like the cover of Fall Out Boy's Infinity on High album.

That was another amazing quality about you Ma', you always allowed us kids to help in any project going on. Even as youngsters, "no" wasn't a word spoken when we wanted to join in. Whether it was cooking and baking with you in the kitchen, painting some room in the house, gardening in the yards… you taught us how to do whatever it was we wanted to help with. Flour on our faces, paint on our clothes, dirt on our hands… no problem, we'll just wash it off.

Bedtime stories… Dad rocked at making up stories, but you were the queen at reading all of my favorite books. From "Where the Wild Things Are" to "If You Give a Mouse a Cookie" to "Don't Forget the Oatmeal Ernie", you knew how to do all of the voices for each individual character and you set the scene perfectly. A show every night at bedtime. There's no better way to end a full day of one's ABC's and 123's than a story read by Ma'. <3

Witty and clever is my middle name… I've been told that I'm quick with the wit, hilarious comments, creative, sarcastic and stubborn (from time to time) and I have finally figured out where I get these fabulous qualities from… You Madam. I have grown into my own self, but when examined under a microscope, bits and pieces of you are embedded into my DNA. I think of you and I like the Gilmore Girls. You being Lorelai and me being Rory. The relationship you and I have is so similar to theirs. Maybe that's why I liked that show so much. We have that close relationship, you've always been my best friend. And I know there's been moments where you've had to play your "Mom" card, but it wasn't too often. I cherish our conversations; I love how we are quick with the movie line references and witty comments. And yes, there have been times where we have been on opposite ends, times where we've been frustrated with each other and moments when silence

117

was had, but in the end hugs and "I'm sorry" were always exchanged and a new day began.

Shake what your Mama gave you... since I was a tiny tot, dancing was encouraged in our house. "The Carrot" and "The Potato" were the first moves you taught me. The "peeling" these veggies move got me shaking my hips and shaking my head. You also enrolled me into Tap and Ballet classes where I learned rhythm, grace and movement. Ballet taught me the gentle beauty of dance while tap taught me a jazzier side to dance. I certainly can shake my hips and bust out a move. I remember when I taught Lu and Zac to dance. They were stiff until I showed them that their hips could move all on their own. Once they mastered that, they became groovin' machines. Tell me what other Mom will crank up the tunes and rock out with her kids in the living room or kitchen.

Snowball! I know you remember the time that I wanted a kitten really bad. I know we had Swift and I loved him. He was the best dog ever, a girl's best friend. But I wanted a kitten too. I begged Dad for one for a whole month straight. He wasn't too big on cats; he was more of a dog lover. My ninth birthday came around and you had a big surprise for me. I never saw it coming. You, being the awesome Mom that you are, had talked Dad into getting me a kitten. You told me to get in the car because we were going out to dinner. We ended up stopping at Pets Mart first and I had just figured that you and Dad needed to pick up some dog food for Swift. I was hanging with Dad near the pet food section when you came over to us holding this adorable tiny kitten.

She was white with black paws, tail and nose. There was a pink ribbon around her neck. I asked whose kitten she was and you told me that she was mine. I jumped up and down in excitement. You carefully handed her over to me to hold, she was so fluffy and soft. I named her Snowball. One of the best birthday gifts ever.

Forgiveness for my stupid moments… so it was my 13th birthday and I was stoked to enter my teenage years. No longer a kid, but not an adult. Sounds great (until it all hits the fan). I came home after school that afternoon and you had planned to take me out for my birthday dinner. As I walked through the door I noticed the look on your face, it was that "you're in deep trouble" look. See, a couple of weeks earlier I had made sure to get the mail before you because I was watching out for the academic warning that I knew was coming. I had ended up with a "D" in English class (on purpose, turns out you work harder to get a bad grade in a class than just doing the work in the first place). I knew that explaining why my grade was a "D" wasn't going to be an easy task. Low grades for me meant that there was something up. Well I ended up grabbing it from the mail before you saw it and instead of destroying the evidence, I hid it. I placed my death in between the pages of a book in my room. Thinking that I was in the clear, I went about my days. I had overlooked one small fact, a three foot fact to be exact. Her name was Alyssa and she liked to go through my stuff when I wasn't in my room. So while I was at school and you were busy cleaning the house, my favorite little monster decided to shop around my room. And guess what she found, my academic warning. Now you would think that she would have taken her crayons and colored all over it, but instead she went the snitch

route and handed it over to you. Being the gracious Ma'
that you are, you held off on the whole grounding me
until the next day. You took the kids and I out for dinner
and dessert. It was a fun night. November 2nd... my
birthday. November 3rd... grounded for a month. Happy
Birthday to me.

Another great quality you possess... an open ear.
Anytime I was in trouble for something you would
always take me aside and ask what was wrong. I wasn't
a trouble making kid (well, at least if I was I was usually
smart enough to cover my tracks). Any attitude, sadness
or problems in school usually had a meaning behind
them. You never just jumped on my case or assumed that
I did whatever I was in trouble for because I was acting
out. We would talk about what was bothering me and
find a solution on how to handle the situation if it should
ever occur again. I was grounded a handful of times
through my young years, but what kid isn't. The worst
part was when you took my art supplies, music and
books away. Boredom and I don't mix, but lessons were
definitely learned.

Those special touches only you know how to do...
Anytime I felt "bleh" due to a cold coming on you
always knew how to make everything better. I love your
homemade chicken noodle soup, it's the absolute
comfort food to cure the sniffles. Cups of hot green tea
with a squeeze of lemon and drizzle of honey soothed
my sore throat. I was always up and running the next
day.

Your special hot chocolate is another specialty of yours that takes me down memory lane with every steamy sip. Hershey's syrup goodness stirred into piping hot milk in a giant mug. Whipped cream, marshmallows and sprinkles floating atop, slow motion melting into the liquid chocolate. It's the holidays in a mug.

Get your game face on and let the smack talking begin!... Some people play games just for the fun entertainment that they bring. Some play for leisure, but not your kids. Nope, I think that we inherited your competitive streak. I know I did. Playing games in our family is a sport. Boggle... Mad Gab... Yahtzee... Pit... Who's It... Bowling on the Wii... All I have to say is bring it on! The second a game is set up the smack talk comes out. And of course a box of tissues is supplied to wipe away any losing tears. I love going round after round with you and the kids. It's always a blast. Oh, and I have yet to prove it, but I know that you cheat at Who's It. The fact that no one can beat you is very suspicious. ;)

You never stomped on any of my ideas, goals or dreams. You never started any conversation with "No" or "Can't". Creativity and hard work were always the cards played to help me achieve my newest project. From Tap and Ballet lessons... art sets so that I could sketch out my imagination... my snare drum days for band during my elementary years... finding a love for cooking which now means we've upgraded from colored pencils and drumsticks to sharp knives and fire... my fascination with the sharpness and beauty of words resulting in my dream of one day becoming an author.

Thank you for never giving up on me, even when I gave up on myself. Thank you for always believing in the person that I've become and showing me the power that unconditional love has. Thank you for being my Ma' <3

I know that this life ain't for the faint of heart, but it's one hell of a beautiful ride. I think that if we would all knock off this whole "labeling" each other bullshit then perhaps our eyes could become truly open to the fact that we're all human... we're all equal. We are all different...all unique and that's how it's supposed to be, that's how God intended it to be. Original human beings coming together to make this life amazing for generations to come.

Live everyday as though it would all end tomorrow. Lead with an open, kind and generous heart. There's a reason why we say "treat others the way you would want to be treated in return". Love your families and friends for the awesomely awkward people that they are and when you find your true love, endlessly hold onto them. Love every good and flawed piece of them because finding the love of your life and spending the rest of your lives together, creating memorable adventures and a family is a precious honor.

I can't resist a good dare and it just so happens that I have one for you. I dare you to be you. Be the person you were placed on this earth to be, whoever that may be. Don't allow outside static to dictate how much of yourself you share with this world. Be 100% original, be 100% you because everybody else is already taken.

Well here we are at the end of my story, did you listen?

Dear You Soundtrack

Till I Collapse
Eminem Ft. Nate Dogg

Airplanes Pt. 2
B.O.B. Ft. Hayley Williams & Eminem

All of Me
John Legend

All the Right Moves
One Republic

Beautiful
Eminem

Berzerk
Eminem

Iris

The Goo Goo Dolls

Blow Me (One Last Kiss)

Pink

Breakdown

Seether

Bring Me to Life

Evanescence

Broken

Seether

Can't Hold Us

Macklemore & Ryan Lewis

3 a.m.

Eminem

Comatose

Skillet

Dance, Dance

Fall Out Boy

Demons

Imagine Dragons

Drink a Beer

Luke Bryan

I'm Not Afraid

Eminem

Space Bound

Eminem

For Blue Skies

Strays Don't' Sleep

Fuckin' Perfect
Pink

Good Life
One Republic

I Miss You
Blink 182

Just One Yesterday
Fall Out Boy

Kryptonite
3 Doors Down

Lose Yourself
Eminem

20 Dollar Nose Bleed
Fall Out Boy

My Songs Know What You Did In the Dark

Fall Out Boy

Phenomenal

Eminem

Kings Never Die

Eminem

Rest of My Life

Ludacris ft. Usher

Run This Town

Jay Z Ft. Rihanna

Sail

Awolnation

Scars

Papa Roach